CHAUCER'S ITALY

CHAUCER'S ITALY

RICHARD OWEN

First published in 2022 by
The Armchair Traveller (an imprint of Haus Publishing Ltd)
4 Cinnamon Row
London SW11 3TW

This paperback edition published in 2023

Cartography produced by ML Design

A CIP catalogue record for this book is available from the British Library

ISBN 978-1-914982-04-0
eISBN 978-1-909961-84-5

Typeset in Garamond by MacGuru Ltd
Printed in the UK by Clays Ltd, Elcograf S.p.A.

www.hauspublishing.com
@HausPublishing

Contents

Europe in the Time of Chaucer (c.1360)

Chaucer and *Ytaille*

Chaucer was a poet; but he never flinched from the life
that was being lived at the moment before his eyes.
—Virginia Woolf

In a collection of stories called the *Decameron*, the Italian
author Giovanni Boccaccio tells of an elderly nobleman in
ancient Greece named Nicostrato, whose young and beautiful
wife Lidia is 'badly served in that one thing in which young
women take most pleasure'. She falls in love with Pirro, a
handsome servant; she then pretends to be ill, gets Nicostrato
and Pirro to carry her into a garden, and asks Pirro to climb
into a pear tree to pick some pears for her. Pirro looks down,
pretends he can see the husband and wife making love, and
says the pear tree must have the power of optical illusion. Old
Nicostrato climbs into the tree to check this out, looks down,
and sees Pirro and his wife making love on the ground. He
climbs down in a fury, calling his wife a 'wicked slut' – but,
by the time he reaches the ground, the lovers have separated.

They convince him that the pear tree is bewitched and must have made him see an illusion.

Some forty years later, Chaucer, writing his *Canterbury Tales,* sets the story in Italy, which is where he probably first read it, or perhaps heard it. In his version, called 'The Merchant's Tale', an elderly bachelor knight in Pavia called January decides to marry 'a young and pretty woman' called May. But January goes blind and, when he takes his wife into the garden, May climbs up into a pear tree to make love to a handsome servant called Damian. January regains his sight and sees Damian 'thrusting away' up in the pear tree – or, as Chaucer puts it, *'and sodeinly anon this Damian gan pullen up the smok and in he throng'.* Old January is furious, calling his wife a whore, but she claims that by 'struggling with a man up a tree', as she had been told to do in a vision, she had cured his blindness, 'as God is my witness'. Because of the magic pear tree, January is imagining things, May says, adding, 'this is all the thanks I get for curing your blindness' and bursting into histrionic tears.

Chaucer never wrote an autobiography. We do not know if the Chaucer who narrates the *Canterbury Tales* – portly, self-effacing, ironic, slightly detached, and sometimes naive or not very bright – is how Chaucer saw himself, how he wanted to be seen, or how he really was seen. A baffled Harry Bailly, 'the Host' of the *Canterbury Tales*, asks Chaucer the narrator at one point, *'What man artow?'*

Brian Helgeland's 2001 film *A Knight's Tale* offers an entertaining but equally unprovable portrait of Chaucer (played by Paul Bettany) as an aspiring writer who has just published the *Book of the Duchess* but is a compulsive gambler who will 'scribble' anything, from summonses and patents of nobility to 'a poem or two'. He acts as announcer at the knights' joust, uses his verbal skills to convince the audience that his 'knight' is a noble Crusader – when, in reality, he is a lower-class impostor – and remarks as the film ends that he must 'write some of this story down' one day.

But the real Chaucer was a man of enormous diplomatic and business experience – canny, witty, and clearly very, very sharp. For Nigel Saul, 'Chaucer was a born storyteller. Does that imply that he was superficial? Certainly not. He was a man of the world, acute and perceptive in his observations.' And Italy was very much part of his world and his perceptions. As Helen Fulton puts it, 'What is striking about Chaucer's use of his Italian sources is the way in which he distributes the borrowed material throughout his work, smelting it, combining it with other elements, and then refashioning it into new gold of his own making.'

I began thinking in earnest about Chaucer and Italy when travelling to Canterbury in January 2020, the year of the 850th anniversary of the murder of Thomas Becket, also known as St Thomas of Canterbury. Chaucer himself is said to have made the pilgrimage to Becket's Canterbury shrine in April 1388, around the time he began the *Canterbury Tales*.

Ours was not exactly a pilgrimage of the kind Chaucer and his pilgrims go on in the Tales: we did not travel by horse, or start from the Tabard Inn in Southwark, and it was January rather than April, 'when sweet showers fall' and 'folk do long to go on pilgrimage'. But we went to Evensong at Canterbury

Cathedral and paid homage to Becket at the spot where he was murdered in 1170 and at the Trinity Chapel, where the place once occupied by Becket's magnificent tomb – a victim of the Reformation, or at least of Henry VIII – is marked by a poignant solitary candle on the floor.

The year 2020 was also the 620th anniversary of Chaucer's death, in October 1400. Although the *Canterbury Tales* end shortly before the pilgrims actually arrive at their destination, a bronze statue of Chaucer was unveiled in Canterbury High Street in 2016, facing the Eastbridge Hospital of St Thomas the Martyr (now an almshouse), where the pilgrims would have spent the night. Over 600 years after their composition, the *Canterbury Tales* still hold their power to entrance and entertain.

The *Canterbury Tales* pilgrims set off for Becket's shrine from London, where Chaucer was born the son of a fourteenth-century wine merchant. The bearded, older Chaucer is depicted in a miniature in Thomas Hoccleve's *The Regiment of Princes* with a rosary in his hand, a pen case round his neck, and a finger pointing at Hoccleve's remark that Chaucer was the '*firste fyndere of oure faire langage*'. He was buried in Westminster Abbey simply because he lived in its grounds in his last years, which led to him being the first writer with a tomb in what became the abbey's Poets' Corner, confirming his status as the father or founder of English literature. But, as a vintner, Chaucer's father traded with Europe, mainly Gascony, the wine country on the French border with Spain. And like his father, and many other Englishmen of the time, Chaucer was deeply involved with Europe in war, diplomacy, and trade – first of all with France (the thoroughly English Wife of Bath is actually based on a figure called La Vieille from the medieval French masterpiece of courtly love, *Roman de la Rose*), but also with Italy (then spelt '*Ytaille*'), which provided Chaucer with his most important literary sources.

As a teenager, Chaucer fought in the Hundred Years' War and was captured near Reims. Later, he almost certainly helped to arrange a royal marriage in Milan as his status rose in the royal court, first under Edward III and then under Richard II, and he certainly made two visits to Italy as a diplomat that had a huge impact on his writing. As Wendy Childs has noted, 'England's Italian contacts were regular and long-standing, particularly through Church links with Rome, but also through political, intellectual, and commercial channels.' The Crown's economy under Edward III largely depended on Italian financiers, especially Matteo Cennini (Matthew Cheyne) and, above all, Walter (Gualtiero) de Bardi, or de Bardes, who became Master of the Mint and a Freeman of the City of London. Chaucer, who would have known both Cennini and de Bardi in London, was sent in 1372–3 on a mission first to Genoa and then to Florence, where the Bardis were based, to negotiate new loans for the king, despite the fact that Edward III had defaulted on earlier debts.

Five years later, Chaucer was again sent to Italy, this time by Edward III's successor, Richard II, on a diplomatic mission to Lombardy. Like the earlier journey to Genoa and Florence, the Lombardy mission took him across the Alps. But then, as David Wallace writes of Chaucer's travels, 'The London culture in which Chaucer spent most of his life was so heterogeneous, so multilingual, so much part of a greater European milieu that the passage to the Continent can hardly have struck him as a journey from familiarity to foreignness.'

Thanks to his dealings with Italian merchants and diplomats as he moved up the social ladder and into court circles, Chaucer spoke Italian and absorbed the writings of celebrated Italian authors who had a profound influence on him – above all, Dante Alighieri, Francesco Petrarch, and Giovanni Boccaccio. As Kara Gaston puts it, 'Chaucer's reading of Italian literature had an effect on him: before he changed it, it changed him.' Petrarch, after all, had been crowned Italian Poet Laureate, had discovered an unknown cache of letters by Cicero at Verona, and had come to be considered 'the father of the Renaissance' for reconciling humanism with his Christian faith. Petrarch became very well known later, in Elizabethan England, not least for his sonnets – yet Chaucer had encountered the work of the great Italian poet 200 years earlier. As for Boccaccio, who came from Certaldo, near Florence, his *Decameron* was without question an inspiration for the *Canterbury Tales,* and Chaucer clearly draws on both Boccaccio's *Teseida* and his *Filostrato.*

As it happened, our own Canterbury trip for the Becket anniversary was our last such journey for some time: it came just before Covid-19 took hold and led to widespread illness, deaths, and lockdowns, all of which revived memories of previous plagues and pandemics – not least the Black Death, which devastated England in 1348, soon after Chaucer's birth. The Black Death, like the Covid-19 pandemic, was international. But it is strongly associated with Italy, not least because it inspired the *Decameron*, in which a young group of seven women and three men meet at the church of Santa Maria Novella in Florence before escaping to take refuge from the plague in a villa in the hills '*due piccole miglia*' ('two short miles') outside the city (thought to be Settignano), where they tell each other a hundred '*novelle*' (tales) to while away the time.

Like England and much of the rest of Europe, Italy lost at least a third of its population because of the plague, which struck Genoa, Venice, Tuscany, and Rome. 'The year 1348 has left us alone and forlorn,' wrote Petrarch. The losses were 'irreparable'. 'Where are our dear friends now?' Petrarch added, in words that sound only too familiar to us after living through Covid-19. 'Where are the beloved faces? Where are the affectionate words, the relaxed and enjoyable conversations? … Time, as they say, has slipped through our fingers.'

The word 'quarantine' is Italian: it comes from '*quaranta giorni*' ('forty days'), the period in Venice for which ships from plague-ridden countries had to wait offshore before being allowed to unload passengers or goods. The 'pestilence' was widely seen in Europe as a sign of God's punishment for human sin. Yet despite – or possibly because of – plague and disease, the fourteenth century was also an era of enterprise and radical social change, with lower-class people rising to high positions and wealth. Chaucer's friend and fellow poet John Gower saw this in negative terms, disapproving of peasants imitating freemen and wearing their clothes: 'Servants are now masters and masters are servants, he who has learned nothing now thinks he knows everything.' In the poem *Piers Plowman*, William Langland, a contemporary of Chaucer's, complains that shoemakers are now able to buy knighthoods. A petition to the Commons in 1363 lamented that 'grooms wear the apparel of craftsmen, craftsmen wear the apparel of gentlemen, and gentlemen wear the apparel of esquires', leading to the first sumptuary laws seeking (largely in vain) to preserve the class system by restricting 'extravagance' in dress, food and drink, and household furnishings.

We tend to see this upheaval as prefiguring the modern world, with England emerging from a time of trauma – a never-ending, debilitating, and hugely expensive war with France; the horror of the Black Death; the Peasants' Revolt – to pave the way for the eighteenth-century Enlightenment. The very word 'medieval' is seen as negative. For Barbara Tuchman in *A Distant Mirror,* the fourteenth century was calamitous, 'a violent, tormented, bewildered, suffering and disintegrating age' comparable to the disastrous wars, atrocities, and genocides of the twentieth century. But it was also a time of castles, Crusaders, chivalry, and cathedrals: as Chris Wickham notes in *Medieval Europe*, we should no longer imagine the Middle Ages to be 'a long dark period of random violence, ignorance, and superstition'. True, it was a period of plague, papal schism, violence, and warfare, but the economy was not destabilised, political structures remained dynamic, and, above all, people became 'more literate and engaged', with a growing sense that 'political discussion and protagonism did not belong only to the traditional elites'. A very common narrative even today, Wickham writes, sees Europe emerging from degradation, ignorance, and poverty to reach its apex in the 'high medieval' twelfth and thirteenth centuries, the post-1350 period then experiencing 'a "waning", with plague, war, schism, and cultural insecurity, until humanism and radical church reform sort matters out again'. But this narrative 'misrepresents the late Middle Ages, and excludes the early Middle Ages and Byzantium entirely'.

In other words, these were not the Dark Ages, as they became known later – not least thanks to Petrarch himself at the dawn of European humanism, and later to Edward Gibbon, who in the eighteenth century viewed the Middle Ages in his seminal work *The History of the Decline and Fall of the Roman Empire* as a 'servile and effeminate age' of superstition. In reality, the later Middle Ages were a time of cosmopolitan contacts and remarkable enterprise and creativity – what Seb Falk has called 'The Light Ages', giving us the first universities, the first eyeglasses, and the first mechanical clocks.

Much the same can be said of Italy. When we think of Italy today, we tend to think of the country unified just over 150 years ago and the wonders of the Italian Renaissance that it inherited – the art and the architecture, not to mention the stunning landscapes, the wine and cuisine, the fashion houses, and the operas. But there was an Italy before that, a divided country of competing duchies and city states that emerged from the ruins of the Roman Empire.

It was a time of vicious rivalry and power struggles, yet by the Middle Ages Italy was beginning to lay the foundations of its culture – its poetry, music, and architecture – despite the chaos created by warring factions in what was still very much a fractured region. For Piero Boitani, it is 'indeed fortunate that Chaucer visited Italy and read Italian literature' in the second half of the fourteenth century, or the trecento, a period 'in which the Middle Ages, classical antiquity, and the roots of modern European culture meet'. In Northern Italy, the rival independent city states built defensive walls and towers, many of which survive today, at least in part. Within these fortifications, local tradesmen and notables formed communes (elected councils) to govern their cities under feudal rule, with the nobility gradually ceding power to the merchant class as the Black Death brought radical social change amid widespread death and destruction.

The maritime republics of Genoa, Venice, Amalfi, Ancona, Pisa, and Gaeta began to emerge as powerful forces. There was growing rivalry, however, between the emperor and the pope, and the city states began to take a stand in favour of one or the other. Those supporting the emperor were known as Ghibellines, an Italian corruption of the name of Waiblingen, a town near Stuttgart that was a power base for the Hohenstaufen dynasty and a key pillar in the Holy Roman Empire, supplying several emperors. By contrast, backers of the pope and Papal States were known as Guelphs, an Italian version of Welf, the name of the dukes of Bavaria, who at first also backed the emperor but later became associated with the papal cause. The division was not clear cut: sometimes – as in Florence – the authorities switched from one side to the other and back again.

Since the city states did not have the resources to maintain their own armies, they depended on mercenary armies under the command of *condottiere* (warlords), the most famous being an Englishman, John Hawkwood, with whom Chaucer negotiated as a royal diplomat. Hawkwood is said to be one of the models for 'The Knight's Tale'.

This, then, is the Italy that Chaucer came to know, travelling to Milan, Genoa, Florence, and probably Pavia. He was not venturing into the unknown, however; on the contrary, medieval Europe was deeply interconnected, an elaborate tapestry of mutual reliance in trade, commerce, and banking, with numerous familial and cultural relationships across boundaries. As David Nicolle writes in his *History of Medieval Life*, 'Medieval Christendom was not a stagnant civilisation awaiting the Renaissance to give Europe new life. It was rapidly changing, varied, and open to new ideas in politics, art, trade, science, even religion, and above all everyday fashions.' Moreover, Nicolle continues, 'everyday life in medieval Europe was rarely as primitive as is popularly believed today'. The 'vast and multi-formed epic poem of English medieval society', wrote Ermanno Barisone, who translated the *Canterbury Tales* into Italian and taught English at Genoa University, was formed at a time when feudalism was 'giving way to national organisation'.

It was a period of dances, horse racing, archery, hunting, bear-baiting, cockfighting, and, of course, knightly tournaments, as well as mystery plays (referred to directly by Alison, the Wife of Bath, in the *Canterbury Tales*). But it was a time, too, of poetic experimentation, civic spectacles, and elaborate art and architecture such as the remarkable Wilton Diptych, a portable diptych of two painted panels now in the National Gallery in London, which shows Richard II kneeling before the Virgin and Child, flanked by John the Baptist and the figures who were then the patron saints of England: Edmund the Martyr and Edward the Confessor.

Local economies were dominated by markets and guilds, with workshops for millers, blacksmiths, potters, and wheel-wrights. Italy led the way in agriculture, with landowners investing in new crops and equipment as well as irrigation and terraced hillsides. Feudal households employed a huge number of people, and the aristocracy moved into manor houses, with an army of relatives and servants and impressive kitchens for roasting and baking.

Far from being dirty or ill-mannered, the emerging middle classes took cleanliness and courtesy very seriously. Literacy and scientific investigation were spreading, and the concept of courtly love took hold, with the idea that men and women could love each other as equals – a concept that was prob-ably more of a literary device than a reality, but which would have none the less seemed outlandish to the ancient Greeks and Romans.

In Chaucer's England, the English language began replac-ing French in the law courts and Parliament, and even in some Church circles with the emergence of the Lollards, who wanted to read the Bible in English rather than Latin. Although printed versions of the Bible in English did not appear until the sixteenth century, the first known Bible in English appeared in manuscript form as early as 1382. It is thought to have been translated by the followers of John Wycliffe (or Wyclif), the leader of the Lollards, and may in part have been the work of Wycliffe himself. The Lollards were later persecuted as heretics, but theirs was in effect an early form of Protestantism. The French – or Anglo-Norman – language remained current in Chaucer's time, some 300 years after the Norman Conquest. But, partly because of the conflicts of the intermittent Hundred Years' War, France and French began to be vilified, and English came to be seen as patriotic. Moreover, as Norman Davis notes, Chaucer 'showed that English could be written with an elegance and power that earlier authors had not attained'.

We tend to see Chaucer as quintessentially English, partly because his characters are familiar English types, from the plain-speaking, garrulous, and much-married Wife of Bath to Harry Bailly, the landlord of the Tabard Inn in Southwark. It is Bailly who leads the pilgrims on the road to Canterbury and suggests they tell stories to pass the time. Originally, the pilgrims were to tell two stories each on the way to Canterbury and two on the way back, but that idea seems to have been abandoned. Similarly, whoever told the best story was to be rewarded with dinner back at the Tabard Inn, but that never happens either. Bailly is referred to throughout as 'The Host' of the pilgrims, and is named in the prologue to 'The Cook's Tale', the fourth story: like Chaucer, who appears as narrator in the *Canterbury Tales* and who was almost certainly a customer at the Tabard Inn and may well have stayed there, Bailly really existed, and he was not only landlord of the inn but also an MP, tax collector, and coroner.

Several of the *Canterbury Tales* are based on French *fabliaux*, fast-paced, often bawdy and slapstick stories. But Chaucer's dealings with Italian merchants, diplomats, aristocrats, and above all writers also brought him into contact with an array of Italian poems and tales to which no other English writer had access. As if to underline the Italian connection, Pier Paolo Pasolini filmed *I Racconti di Canterbury* in 1972, with himself – quill in hand – as Chaucer. The film was part of a trilogy, preceded by Pasolini's version of Boccaccio's *Decameron* (1971) and followed by his *A Thousand and One Nights* (1974).

The once-accepted notion that Chaucer's life can be divided into three parts – French, Italian, and English – has long been discounted: Italy stayed with him throughout his life as a writer. Marion Turner noted in *Chaucer: A European Life*:

> Italian poetry utterly transformed the kind of poet that Chaucer was. That is not to say that he abandoned French or Latin sources. Indeed, Italian literature was itself born out of careful reading of texts in these languages. However, the poetry of Dante and Boccaccio became Chaucer's principal inspiration for the majority of his poetic career.

For Alison, the Wife of Bath, Dante is '*the wise poete of Florence*', while in 'The Monk's Tale' he is '*the grete poete of Ytaille*'. To quote Warren Ginsberg, Chaucer was 'the only poet of his day who visited Italy and created poems that were based on works by its most renowned authors'. In *Dante's British Public*, Nick Havely describes the purchase of a copy of Dante's *Divina Commedia* by an Italian from a fellow Italian in London, noting that the manuscript must have arrived through Italian merchant shipping, and commenting that 'books of this sort could have arrived by similar means even earlier, for example through merchants from Italian towns such as Lucca who had been trading in London around Chaucer's time'.

Chaucer was the first to translate a sonnet by Petrarch into English, and Boccaccio in particular was a profound influence: Chaucer's *Troilus and Criseyde* is indebted to Boccaccio's *Filostrato*; the Italian's *Teseida* is a source for 'The Knight's Tale'; and the story of Menedon in the *Filocolo* is a model for 'The Franklin's Tale'. Chaucer acknowledges Petrarch as his source for 'The Clerk's Tale', the story of the superhuman patience of Griselda as a sorely tried wife. But the original story was in Boccaccio's *Decameron,* and another version (in which Griselda is renamed Constantina) was told by Giovanni Sercambi in his *Novelle*, a collection of tales told by citizens of Lucca (where Sercambi was an apothecary) fleeing the plague, as in the *Decameron.*

In Chaucer's *Canterbury Tales*, 'The Monk's Tale', 'The Knight's Tale', 'The Shipman's Tale', and 'The Franklin's Tale' are all clearly based on Boccaccio's *Decameron*, and like the *Decameron* they are both bawdy and serious. Oddly, Chaucer never once mentions Boccaccio by name, even though he cites Petrarch directly. Nor does he ever quote directly from the *Decameron*, even though he must have either had a copy or at least seen and memorised it: as we shall see, my own view is that Chaucer met Boccaccio, possibly in Milan and almost certainly in Florence.

Chaucer's life as a courtier and diplomat was intimately linked to Europe: King Edward III's wife was Queen Philippa of Hainault, which was then part of the Holy Roman Empire and is now on the border between France and Belgium; Queen Anne of Bohemia was the wife of Edward III's successor, Richard II, and was the daughter of Charles IV, the Holy Roman Emperor; and Chaucer's own wife was called Philippa, like the queen, and, like her, she came from Hainault. And when Chaucer travelled to Genoa with Italian merchants to negotiate a trade arrangement allowing Genoans to have their own port on the southern English coast, he did so as a supporter and aide of John of Gaunt, son of Edward III – and later Chaucer's brother-in-law – who was at odds with those London merchants who saw the Italians as a threat to their wool-trade monopoly.

On one hand, 'Italy' in Chaucer's time was still more of a geographical entity than a political one, and the inland cities were dominated by ruling dynasties – the della Scalas in Verona, the Viscontis in Milan, the Gonzagas in Mantua, the d'Estes in Ferrara. The South was dominated by the Kingdom of Naples, while in the middle the Papal States were centred on Rome but stretched to Bologna and Ferrara in the North and Frosinone in the South. On the other hand, Italy has always been made up of rival areas with fiercely independent local identities, from Sicily and Sardinia to Lombardy and the Veneto, yet the concept of *Italianità* ('Italianness') was as widespread in Italy in the Middle Ages as it is in our own day. In his *Canzoniere*, the collection of sonnets addressed to his idealised love, Laura, Petrarch refers to '*Italia mia*' or '*nostro stato*' ('our nation'), defining Italy as the land with three great rivers: the Tiber, the Arno, and the Po.

The saying that *un inglese italianato e un diavolo incarnato* ('an Italianised Englishman is a devil incarnate') is said to have been coined for John Hawkwood. In a sense, Chaucer, too, was *un inglese italianato.* But his encounter with continental Europe did not begin when he crossed the English Channel for the first time as a teenager, or when he crossed the Alps later as a young man: it began even earlier, in London.

1

Italy on the Thames

Chaucer's date of birth is not recorded. Testifying in a dispute between two knights at the Court of Chivalry in 1386, Chaucer said he was aged 'forty years and more' and had borne arms for twenty-seven years. This puts his birth sometime in the early 1340s, most probably in 1342 and almost certainly in London, where his family lived and ran a business.

He was born into dramatic times – just five years after the start of the Hundred Years' War and only six years before the Black Death arrived in England. By the time Chaucer appeared in the world, the Plantagenet Edward III had been on the throne for some fifteen years: he came to power at the age of fourteen, after his mother, Isabella of France, and her lover, Roger Mortimer, had mounted a coup against his father, the disastrously ineffectual Edward II. Unlike his father, Edward III reigned for half a century, giving England at least a measure of political stability at a time of war and disease.

Though there is no documentary evidence, Chaucer is thought to have been educated at a grammar school, possibly the almonry grammar school at St Paul's. He was certainly well educated and socially ambitious: for most boys growing up in London in the mid-fourteenth century, the court of Edward III must have seemed pretty remote, yet Chaucer became a page in the service of Elizabeth de Burgh, Duchess of Clarence, Countess of Ulster, and wife of the king's second son, Lionel of Antwerp. The word 'page' tends to suggest a humble post involving household chores, from running errands to making beds. In fact, in the Middle Ages it was very far from humble – being made a page was the first step on the road to knighthood, or at least the rank of squire, and it amounted to an apprenticeship in the arts of chivalry and heraldry. The effect was to put Chaucer at the heart of the royal court: by 1367, when he was about twenty-five, Chaucer had risen to be a courtier to the king himself. How did this come about? Unlikely as it may seem, the answer appears to lie in the wine trade.

Chaucer's family name is derived from the French '*chausseur*', one meaning of which is shoemaker. But Chaucer's father and grandfather were not shoemakers; they were both London vintners, and several previous generations had been merchants in Ipswich. St Martin Vintry, their church in Vintry Ward, just north of Southwark Bridge, was the church of London wine merchants, St Martin of Tours being the patron saint of the Vintners' Company. As a soldier in the Roman cavalry in Gaul in the fourth century, Martin cut his cloak in half to share it with a starving beggar at Amiens. He became a travelling priest and is said to have brought a monastery vineyard in the Loire Valley back to life through prayer after his donkey munched all the vines, grapes, and stems during the night. His feast day, 11 November, was formerly the feast of

Bacchus. Sadly, St Martin Vintry was destroyed in the Great Fire of London in 1666 and was never rebuilt; intriguingly, we are told it had an altar dedicated to St Thomas Becket of Canterbury, or St Thomas Martyr, which the young Chaucer surely must have seen.

The London of Chaucer's time had a population of around 50,000–70,000 concentrated in the City, on the north bank of the Thames, with Westminster across the fields to the west being the site of both the abbey and the royal seat of government. London's population was growing, with immigrants coming from all over England – partly due to the social disruption caused by the Black Death – and from Europe. French, Dutch, and German were often to be heard in London streets – along with Italian.

As Wendy Childs has observed, Italians in London were well integrated:

> They traded, leased houses, brought up families, lent money, acted as brokers, recovered debts, acted as witnesses and sureties for Italians and Englishmen, sat on juries to hear cases according to law merchant, stored valuables in their safe-rooms, held royal offices, supplied luxuries for the royal household, and went abroad for the king. They sued and were sued in English courts, and were imprisoned in English prisons.

Frances Stonor Saunders elaborates in her biography of John Hawkwood:

Whatever people desired to buy, Italy offered for sale:
wheat, oil, wine, honey; armour from Milan, white linen
from Genoa, fustian from Cremona, scarlet silks and
brocades from Lucca, silver belts and gold wedding rings,
white, blue and undyed woollen cloth, sewing-thread and
silk curtains and curtain-rings, tablecloths and napkins
and large bath-towels, painted panels from Florence.

Church and university links with Italy were strong: several
of the bishops in medieval England were Italian, including a
series of Bishops of Worcester, and there were Italian friars in
London. Several of the physicians at the court of Edward III
were also Italian.

The Italians in London were not always popular: in the
mid-thirteenth century, the Benedictine monk and chronicler
Matthew Paris commented in his *Chronica Majora* on the size
of the houses being bought up by Italian merchants. As Nick
Havely notes, Chaucer's fellow poet John Gower referred
to 'Lombard foreigners' who 'in order to deceive put on an
appearance of being our friends, yet beneath that they have
set their hearts on plundering us of our silver and gold'. Yet,
despite this hostility towards 'alien' traders buying up quantities of Cotswold wool, Havely affirms that 'there is substantial
evidence about the presence of Italian residents of various
classes in the major cities of Chaucer's England'.

For Marion Turner, Chaucer's upbringing in the City of
London gave him 'the opportunity to mix with Italians and
to learn the language', a skill 'that was to transform not only
Chaucer's own poetry but English literature'. Growing up

'in a wealthy merchant's house on the bank of the Thames, watching the ships come in bringing products from all over the world, provided a cosmopolitan childhood for the boy who was to become an exceptionally cosmopolitan poet'. Robert Edwards has even described Vintry Ward as Chaucer's 'first Italian place'.

Vintry Ward was – and still is – on the Thames. One of twenty-five wards in the City of London, it is bounded by the Thames to the south, Cannon Street to the north, College Hill to the east and Lambeth Hill and Distaff Lane to the west. The church of St James Garlickhythe – named after the nearby medieval dock for wine and garlic – made it a departure point for pilgrimages to Santiago de Compostela in Spain, the shrine of St James. In Chaucer's time, Vintry was a densely populated area of tenements and shops but also larger houses for the well-to-do, with courtyards and gardens. At the docks, wine from the Continent – above all, Gascony – was unloaded together with cloth, skins, fish, and spices, and cargoes of English wool were sent out. Trade with Europe thrived here, against a London backdrop of church bells, horses and carts, and street sellers of spices and peppers.

Relations with Flanders in particular were tied to the wool trade, since Flanders' principal cities relied heavily on textile production and England supplied much of the raw material they needed. As a symbol of the importance of the wool trade, Edward III ordered his Lord Chancellor to sit on a woolsack – now the seat of the Speaker in the House of Lords, a square cushion covered in red cloth (though the wool inside has been repeatedly replaced and was last restuffed in 1938).

The Chaucers lived in Thames Street, today a major thoroughfare divided into Upper and Lower Thames Street, separated from the river by buildings and lined with soulless office blocks, thanks to the wartime Blitz and post-war development. But in the fourteenth century it ran along the riverside, a bustling street with wharves and docks, crowded with shops and traders. In *The Waste Land*, T. S. Eliot describes it in the twentieth century yet still captures something of its past:

> O City city, I can sometimes hear
> Beside a public bar in Lower Thames Street,
> The pleasant whining of a mandoline
> And a clatter and a chatter from within
> Where fishmen lounge at noon: where the walls
> Of Magnus Martyr hold
> Inexplicable splendour of Ionian white and gold.

The spacious Chaucer family house – thought to have been at what is now 177 or 179 Upper Thames Street – bordered the Walbrook, a river that was used as a constant conduit to the Thames for sewage. The streets, by contrast, were regularly cleaned of both human and animal excrement. Society was dominated by the king and nobility, with the landowning gentry the next stage down on the social ladder. But there was also a growing class of craftsmen and merchants. In June 1380, Chaucer referred to himself as '*me Galfridum Chaucer, filium Johannis Chaucer, Vinetarii, Londonie*' ('Geoffrey Chaucer, son of John Chaucer, vintners, London'). John Chaucer's marriage added to his status, since his wife, Agnes Copton – Chaucer's mother – inherited a number of properties in 1349, including twenty-four shops in London, from an uncle.

The Black Death, which struck London in the autumn of 1348, had a devastating effect in the narrow and overcrowded streets. It had many of the features of later plagues, including the Covid-19 pandemic that began in 2020 – the spread of infections; deaths and burials; panic followed by resignation; escapism or adjustment to a new way of life – but was far more deadly, there being no vaccines to counteract it. Chaucer's parents, however, not only survived the plague but were among those who actually benefited from it, partly because they inherited property from relatives who died but also because of the business opportunities and social mobility that arose in the aftermath of the disease. It was John Chaucer's appointment in 1347 as deputy butler to the king at the port of Southampton that gave Geoffrey Chaucer such a grand start in life. As a result, the family moved to Southampton for two and a half years during the plague, and returned to find London with its population decimated and wages and prices higher – to their advantage.

Southampton was not exactly left unscathed by the Black Death – on the contrary, the plague is thought to have arrived first at the port by sea and to have spread through England from there. But the Chaucer family pulled through, and Chaucer senior's posting put him in charge of the royal wine supplies and involved links with both the court in London and traders on the Continent.

The first of the 'Chaucer Life-Records' appears about ten years later, in 1357, in the household accounts of Elizabeth de Burgh, to whom Chaucher had become page through his father's connections. He could have followed his father into the wine trade; instead, he became part of the royal court itself. The countess was betrothed to Prince Lionel in 1342, when she was only ten and Lionel was only four. Early weddings for dynastic reasons were common in the Middle Ages, and when Elizabeth turned twenty and Lionel was fourteen they were married. The teenage Chaucer's position in their court brought him into royal circles, where he was to remain for the rest of his life.

Derek Brewer notes in his life of Chaucer:

> Geoffrey Chaucer makes his first appearance on the stage of history with a characteristic combination of vagueness and sharp outline. He is between twelve and seventeen and smallish, wearing shoes, black and red breeches and a 'paltock' or short cloak, bought in London on 4 April 1357 and costing seven shillings in all, the gift of his lady, the Countess Elizabeth of Ulster.

These remarkable details only emerged in 1851, from parchments that had been used to line bindings in manuscripts acquired by the British Museum. They show that the young Chaucer was not a lowly servant in the royal household but more of a *valettus* (valet) or esquire, given important errands to run; as Paul Strohm puts it, 'One does not wear a paltock to grub out the stables.' Indeed, 'the first time that Geoffrey Chaucer appears before us in documentary records he does not appear as a poet, customs officer, diplomat or soldier,' says

Marion Turner. 'Instead he steps off the page as a fashion plate, dressed to the nines in clothes so breathtakingly fashionable and daring that contemporary commentators condemned them as causing the wrath of God to descend on England in the shape of the plague.' Young men like Chaucer went about 'in short tunics and long, two-coloured leggings or tights, laced up together provocatively in such a way as to emphasise the genitals indecently'.

The adolescent Chaucer, in other words, had been catapulted into a royal household interested in bold style and trendsetting. For Chaucer, it was the first step on a ladder that would lead to his later roles as a courtier, royal emissary, controller of the wool trade, and clerk of the King's Works – making one wonder if William Langland was perhaps playing on the French meaning of Chaucer's surname in a dig at his fellow author when, towards the end of the fourteenth century, he wrote in *Piers Plowman* that mere shoemakers were nowadays becoming knights.

It was the Hundred Years' War that gave Chaucer his first experience of the realities of life when he was still only a teenager. The war (a sporadic series of conflicts with France that actually lasted well over a hundred years) started in May 1337, when Philip VI of France decided to take back the Duchy of Aquitaine (which had been English since the twelfth century, when Eleanor of Aquitaine married Henry II), including Gascony. Edward III responded by challenging Philip's right to the French throne and claiming it for himself, on the grounds that his French mother, Isabella, had been the daughter of the French King Philip IV.

In 1340 Edward formally assumed the title 'King of France and the French Royal Arms'. On 22 June that year, Edward and his fleet sailed from England, and the French fleet assumed a defensive formation off the port of Sluis (then spelt 'Sluys'). The English fleet pretended it was withdrawing but then turned and attacked with the wind and sun behind it. The French fleet was almost completely destroyed in what became celebrated as the Battle of Sluys.

England dominated the English Channel for the rest of the war, preventing French invasion. At this point, Edward III's funds ran out, and the war probably would have ended, but in 1341 conflict over Brittany began the War of the Breton Succession, in which Edward backed John of Montfort and Philip backed Charles of Blois. In July 1346, Edward mounted a major invasion across the channel, landing in Normandy at St Vaast. The English army captured the completely unguarded Caen in just one day, surprising the French.

Philip mustered a large army to oppose Edward, but the Battle of Crecy was a disaster for the French, thanks to the skills of English longbowmen and the fact that the French king allowed his army to attack before it was ready. Edward proceeded north unopposed and besieged the city of Calais, capturing it in 1347. Calais would remain under English control for over 200 years.

In 1355 Edward's son and namesake, the Prince of Wales, later known as the Black Prince, attacked Carcassonne and Narbonne, leading to the Battle of Poitiers in 1356, when the French King Jean II (or John II) was captured. The young Chaucer became involved four years later, when Edward invaded France for the third and last time in 1359, still hoping to seize the French throne for himself and be crowned at the cathedral city of Reims.

The king and his forces landed at Calais in October 1359. Chaucer, by now aged sixteen or seventeen, was part of Duke Lionel's company, which served under the Black Prince and marched through France in late autumn 1359, in rain and mud. At the end of November, they besieged Reims for five weeks, but the citizens reinforced the city's defences, and the French fought back.

Chaucer was at Rethel, on the river Aisne in the Ardennes, almost 40 km from Reims, when he was captured. We can only imagine how it felt to be in enemy hands – though perhaps Chaucer knew (or at least hoped) that as a member of the royal entourage he could expect to be the subject of a bargain. In the event, Edward paid 16 pounds for his ransom – a considerable sum, equivalent to as much as 12,000 pounds in today's money – and the young valet was released. It was to this experience that Chaucer referred in his testimony to the Court of Chivalry years later, when on 15 October 1386 he gave evidence in the dispute between the Scrope and Grosvenor families over which of them had the right to bear the coat of arms *azure, a bend or* ('a blue field with a golden band') – this testimony, as we have seen, gives us the only clue to Chaucer's date of birth. He backed the Scropes, who won the case.

Edward's military campaign continued (without Chaucer), but not for long: the king moved on towards Paris but retreated after a few skirmishes in the suburbs. Disaster then struck at Chartres with a hailstorm that caused over 1,000 English deaths. This devastated Edward's army, forcing him to negotiate with the French. At Bretigny, near Chartres, in May 1360, in return for more lands including Calais and the whole of Aquitaine, Edward renounced his claim to Normandy, Brittany, Touraine, Anjou, and Maine, agreed to reduce John II's ransom by a million crowns and – crucially – gave up his ambition to be crowned king of France.

Chaucer was at Calais in October 1360 for the ratification of the Treaty of Bretigny. The most important event for him at this time, however, was not the struggle for control of France but his courtship of Philippa de Roet, whom he married in September 1366, when he was about twenty-four. Like many young men (then as now), Chaucer had a wild side: he is, for example, recorded as having beaten a Franciscan friar in Fleet Street. But, as Derek Brewer has noted, the Middle Ages were often violent times, and Chaucer as a young man in his early twenties was no doubt 'brimming with life and energy' and was at the same time both 'passionate and sensitive'.

He was, moreover, a rising courtier and the son of a prosperous merchant. We know nothing of his courtship of de Roet, but it was clearly the result of his presence in the royal entourage – and it reinforced his rise up the social ladder. De Roet, after all, was not only lady-in-waiting to Edward III's queen, Philippa of Hainault – who may have arranged the marriage herself – but also the sister of Katherine Swynford (née de Roet), later the mistress of the powerful John of Gaunt and eventually his third wife.

De Roet, moreover, was from Hainault, as was Queen Philippa herself. Hainault is now a Belgian province on the border between Belgium and France, with Mons and Charleroi among its main towns, but in the Middle Ages it was an important – and wealthy – part of the Holy Roman Empire. De Roet's father, Paon (or Gilles) de Roet, was a Hainault knight who came to England as part of Queen Philippa's entourage, and who carried out important missions for Edward III. During the siege of Calais in 1347, it was Paon de Roet who, on Queen Philippa's instructions, conducted the condemned burghers of Calais to safety after they had offered their lives to save their fellow citizens.

Hainault thus became as important to Chaucer as London was. It is uncertain how many children Chaucer and Philippa de Roet had, but it appears there were at least three: Thomas, Elizabeth, and Lewis. Thomas later had an illustrious career as chief butler to four kings, envoy to France, and speaker of the House of Commons; by contrast, Elizabeth became a nun at St Helen's Bishopsgate, close to Chaucer's later lodgings at Aldgate, and then at Barking Abbey (of which only one gatehouse, the Curfew Tower, now survives). As for Lewis, Chaucer is known to have written his *Treatise on the Astrolabe* for his '*litel sone*' ('little son').

There may have been another daughter, Agnes, who was an attendant at Henry IV's coronation in October 1399. Chaucer's granddaughter Alice (the daughter of Thomas) married the future Duke of Suffolk, so that within four generations, as Ruth Evans has noted, 'the Chaucer family progressed from merchant vintners to aristocrats [in a] textbook example of the upward social mobility that characterises the later fourteenth century'.

Chaucer and his new wife moved up the social ladder, with the future poet becoming a member of the royal court of Edward III on 20 June 1367 as a yeoman or esquire, a position that could entail a wide variety of government tasks. His wife also received a pension for court employment. What is most striking, however, is Chaucer's close relationship with one of the most influential men of his time – John of Gaunt, Duke of Lancaster, son of Edward III. Immensely rich, John was the founder of the House of Lancaster, which would later provide kings of England (starting with John's own son Henry Bolingbroke, Henry IV) in rivalry with the House of York – which can also be traced back to John through Joan Beaufort, his daughter by Katherine Swynford. Like Chaucer, John of Gaunt had strong links to Europe: he was born in Ghent (now in Belgium), hence his name ('Ghent' becoming 'Gaunt' in English). He and Chaucer could hardly have been closer: John's children by Swynford were Chaucer's nieces and nephews. Chaucer's *Book of the Duchess* was written – in English – in honour of John's first wife, Blanche of Lancaster, who married John (the 'Man in Black' in Chaucer's poem) in 1359 at Reading Abbey. Her wealth provided the basis of his fortune, and she died in September 1368. Chaucer, by now aged almost thirty, may well have performed the work either at Blanche's funeral at St Paul's or at John's London palace, the Savoy. In it, the poet dreams of a black knight who tells him he is mourning grievously after the death of his love, a lady called White (her name alluding to Blanche). The poem refers to *'a long castel with walles white / Be Seynt Johan, on a ryche hil'*; the phrase *'long castel'* is a reference to Lancaster (also called 'Loncastel' and 'Longcastell'), while '*walles white*' is thought to be a reference to Blanche. '*Seynt Johan*' was John's name-saint, and '*ryche hil*' is a reference to Richmond, one of John's titles being Earl of Richmond.

Chaucer's short poem 'Fortune', believed to have been written in the 1390s, refers to his '*beste frend*', thought by some to mean Richard II but by others to mean John of Gaunt. If the latter, this would make it improbable that – as some Chaucer scholars in the past have suggested – Chaucer's wife, Philippa de Roet, was (like her sister Katherine Swynford) one of John's mistresses, and that either Thomas or Lewis Chaucer was in reality John's son rather than Chaucer's. John died in 1399, a year before Chaucer, and was buried alongside his first wife, Blanche, in an elaborate tomb in the choir of St Paul's Cathedral. Sadly, the tomb – like St Martin Vintry, Chaucer's parish church – was lost in the Great Fire of London in 1666 and is nowadays remembered only in a wall memorial.

2

The Milan Wedding

In 1366 – the year of his marriage to Philippa de Roet – Chaucer was granted 'safe conduct' by Charles II of Navarre in Spain, originally the Kingdom of Pamplona, from February to May. The reason is unclear: it may have been his first diplomatic mission on behalf of Edward III and John of Gaunt, or possibly it was for a journey to Santiago de Compostela, Chaucer's first experience of pilgrimage. Spain and England were often at odds in Edward's reign, but there were also periods of peace – and trade.

What is more likely is that two years later, in 1368, Chaucer was involved in arrangements for the marriage in Milan of his patron, Edward's son Lionel of Antwerp, now aged twenty-nine, to Violante Visconti, aged just thirteen. Violante Visconti was the daughter of Galeazzo II Visconti, who, as lord of Milan and head of the powerful Visconti clan together with his brother Bernabò, controlled much of northern Italy. Galeazzo II Visconti's wife – Violante Visconti's mother – was Bianca of Savoy, and it is thought that Amedeo, the Count of Savoy, played a role in negotiating Violante Visconti's marriage to Lionel.

Lionel's first wife, Elizabeth de Burgh, had died from unknown causes at the age of thirty-one in Dublin in 1363, just over ten years after their youthful marriage. Lionel then became Duke of Clarence, so named because his late wife had the rights to the manor of Clare on the River Stour near Bury St Edmunds in Suffolk, and also Earl of Ulster, having inherited Elizabeth's Irish lands and possessions. Lionel duly became governor of Ireland, but he found it difficult to assert his authority in Ireland and, after holding a parliament at Kilkenny, he returned to England.

As a member of the royal entourage, Chaucer would almost certainly have been party to the negotiations and preparations for the wedding at the Basilica of Santa Maria Maggiore in Milan; there is no documentary evidence that he attended the wedding himself, but it is entirely likely that he was present either at the wedding or at the lengthy celebrations that followed – and that in Milan he probably first met Petrarch, and perhaps Boccaccio.

Journeying to Milan with a huge royal party, Lionel was received in great state in both France and Italy, and he was married to Violante Visconti in Milan in June 1368. Some months were then spent in festivities. Chaucer is known to have been granted leave to pass through Dover in 1368 – but not until July, a month after the Milan wedding. On the other hand, as Wendy Childs has noted, the records show that knights in Lionel's entourage expected to be away for at least a year because of the marriage, and Lionel organised sufficient shipping across the Channel to carry nearly 500 men and over 1,200 horses.

In 1367 Chaucer had been made an esquire in the service of the king and awarded twenty marks per annum for life. David Wallace in *Premodern Places* notes that Chaucer 'passed at Dover' on 17 July 1368, with two horses, expenses, and a permit lasting until the end of October, and so 'could have been out of the country for up to 106 days. He might have gone only as far as Calais, where Henry le Scrope had recently assumed governership, *or he might (easily, in this time frame) have travelled to Italy*' (my italics). Karen Gross agrees:

> [Sceptics] dismiss as an old yarn the hypothesis that Chaucer may have met Petrarch in Milan in 1368 at the wedding celebrations of his old patron Lionel, Duke of Clarence, [but] the truth is that Chaucer might very well have been in Milan just after the party started: Chaucer received a permit from Dover to cross to the Continent on July 17, 1368, and his business and whereabouts are unknown. He may have stayed on the Continent for as a long as 106 days, ample time to journey south to visit his old patron and belatedly join in the elaborate wedding festivities, which continued unabated for four months, halted only by Lionel's illness.

Frances Stonor Saunders has no doubt that 'travelling to Lombardy from England in Lionel's court was Geoffrey Chaucer, a junior esquire of the royal household who had recently been awarded an annuity of twenty marks for life'.

What would Chaucer have seen in Milan? The modern city is largely eighteenth and nineteenth century in origin. But in Roman times Milan, known as Mediolanum, became the unofficial capital of the Western Roman Empire. The famous Edict of Milan, issued by Emperor Constantine in AD 313, ensured tolerance for all faiths in the empire, thus paving the way for Christianity to become its official religion. The impressive foundations of the once-vast imperial palace of the emperor Maximianus can still be seen in Via Brisa, not far from the great Gothic basilica where Lionel and Visconti's wedding was celebrated.

Other examples of the Roman and medieval Milan that Chaucer would have encountered survive, including the basilicas of San Simpliciano and San Nazaro in Brolo (said to contain the relics of the Apostles John, Andrew, and Thomas), as well as two of the ancient city gates, the Porta Nuova and the Porta Ticinese, close to the impressive sixteen Corinthian columns of the colonnade of San Lorenzo.

The nearby Basilica of San Lorenzo, built in the fourth century on an artificial hill above marshy ground, remained a symbol of Roman Milan in the Middle Ages and a centre of Christian ritual, especially on Palm Sunday, when it was held to represent the Mount of Olives. The Basilica of St Ambrose was – and is – another surviving monument of Roman Milan, built for St Ambrose, then the Bishop of Milan, at the end of the fourth century, not long after the Edict of Milan. Ambrose, now one of the four Western Doctors of the Church together with Augustine, Jerome, and Gregory the Great, was noted for his insistence on regional and liturgical flexibility, coining the phrase 'when in Rome, do as the Romans do'.

Above all, perhaps, given the purpose of his visit, Chaucer

would have been impressed by the giant warlike equestrian statue of Bernabò Visconti, the bride's uncle, sculpted in marble five years earlier by Bonino da Campione and placed – bizarrely – over the high altar of San Giovanni in Conca (it is now in the Castello Sforzesco in Milan). Two small female statues representing Strength and Justice support Bernabò on his horse, but they are clearly dominated by the arrogantly masculine figure of the Visconti boss, armed with a sword and staring straight ahead.

The autocratic Visconti dynasty that ruled Milan in the Middle Ages had been founded in the thirteenth century by Ottone Visconti, the Archbishop of Milan. The Visconti family was not exactly benign: it was headed jointly in the fourteenth century by three brothers, Matteo, Galeazzo II, and Bernabò, until 1355, when Galeazzo II and Bernabò had their brother Matteo murdered and divided power between them.

For Chaucer, the Viscontis were the '*scourge of Lumbardie*', as he put it in 'The Monk's Tale', or '*tirauntz of Lumbardye*' (prologue to the *Legend of Good Women*). On Galeazzo II's death in August 1378 – a decade after the marriage of Lionel of Antwerp and Violante Visconti – Bernabò took sole control and proved to be brutal, coarse-humoured, and boastful of his cruelties. In one of Bernabò's milder moments, when the pope had served both him and Galeazzo II with excommunication papers in 1373 for opposing the Papal States, Bernabò made the two papal delegates eat the parchment, the seal, and the silk cord that was rolled around them before he would release them. 'Don't you know I am pope and emperor as well as lord of all my lands?' he demanded.

In 1385 Galeazzo II's son, Giangaleazzo, mounted a coup against his uncle, who was poisoned in prison in the massive Visconti castle at Trezzo that Bernabò had himself had constructed – an event that Chaucer evidently remembered, since the Monk in the *Canterbury Tales* recalls it:

> I sing of you, Bernabò Visconti, lord of Milan, scourge of Lombardy, lover of ease and delight. Why should I not recount your misfortunes? You were raised high only to be brought down by your brother's son. Your nephew cast you into prison, and there you died.

Chaucer (or the Monk) adds, perhaps diplomatically, 'I do not know the reason. I do not know the killer.' The castle at Trezzo on the River Adda, some 30 km from Milan, still exists and is open to visitors.

Milan itself at the time of Lionel's wedding was dominated by two huge palaces, the residences of the two Visconti brothers. Galeazzo II's palace – at least as reconstructed by the Sforza family, who succeeded the Viscontis as rulers of Milan in the fifteenth century – is still in Milan. The Castello Sforzesco, as it is known, now houses Milan's civic museums, including a museum of musical instruments, an Egyptian museum, an ancient art museum, and masterpieces by Michelangelo, Canaletto, Tiepolo, Titian, and Andrea Mantegna, as well as Bernabò's equestrian statue.

Bernabò's palace, by contrast, is long gone, as is most of the elaborately frescoed Visconti church, San Giovanni in Conca, which Bernabò had incorporated into his palace and in which his statue once stood. It is hard now to imagine the impact this church must have made, with its rose window and 24 m high bell tower. The church passed in the sixteenth century to the Carmelite order, which used it as an observatory. But it was then deconsecrated and eventually closed by successive Austrian and French occupiers of Milan, until it finally met an ignominious end in the nineteenth century, when Via Mazzini was driven through it as part of Milan's expansion and urban development. The remains were demolished in 1949, and the Protestant Waldensians, who by now owned what was left, erected the old facade on their new church – known as the Chiesa Valdese San Giovanni in Conca – nearby in Via Francesco Sforza, where it can still be seen. All that is otherwise left of Bernabò's once-magnificent church is the Romanesque crypt, reached via a descending flight of steps in the middle of Piazza Giuseppe Missori, where a mullioned window and some archaeological discoveries are displayed.

For Chaucer, however, the palaces of both Galeazzo II and Bernabò Visconti would have been truly impressive, as would the Palazzo del Broletto (later the Palazzo Reale or Royal Palace, now a civic museum and art gallery), built by their despotic uncle Azzone Visconti. Chaucer, as John Larner has noted, would have seen there an enclosure with 'rare animals and birds' including lions, bears, and ostriches, and, in the cloistered courtyard, a fountain 'surmounted by an angel with the banner of the Visconti'.

The ducal chapel was the church of San Gottardo in Corte, originally dedicated to the Blessed Virgin Mary but renamed after the patron saint of those suffering from gout, as Azzone

Visconti did. It can still be seen and visited, with its octagonal bell tower and chiming clock. The wedding of Lionel and Violante Visconti took place at the Basilica of Santa Maria Maggiore, which dated to the fourth century. Built during the time of St Ambrose, the basilica gave way eighteen years later to the duomo on the same site.

Lionel's party – including 457 men armed with bows and shields – travelled from Dover to Paris via Calais and Abbeville, according to the poet and chronicler Jean Froissart, who was in Lionel's entourage. They then moved on to Chambery in the French Alps – the seat of the House of Savoy, Visconti's mother's family – and then to Pavia, before arriving in Milan. Here they were met at the city gate, the Porta Ticinese, by eighty ladies of the Visconti court all wearing the same outfit: close-fitting scarlet tunics called cote-hardies, with gilded belts and sleeves of white cloth embroidered in trefoil designs. They were followed by thirty knights and thirty squires on horseback led by Galeazzo II Visconti, the bride's father.

The wedding took place nine days later, on Monday 5 June, with Oldrado the Bishop of nearby Novara performing the marriage and conducting high mass afterwards. The festivities for fifty-seven guests began with two vast separate tables for men and women on the Piazza dell'Arengo ('Place of the Harangue', now the Piazza del Duomo), serving thirty courses including beef, suckling pigs, eels, crabs, calves, partridges, quails, ducks, herons, and trout, all covered with a sauce of egg, saffron, flour, and gold leaf and washed down with quantities of wine. The gifts, brought in and presented after each course, included greyhounds with velvet collars, brass buckles, and silk leashes; goshawks wearing silver buttons adorned with the arms of Galeazzo II and Lionel; and horses with reins of velvet and bridles of gold. And that was just the start: the celebrations and gifts of horses, dogs, hawks, jewels and gold, and silk cloth went on for months, as was traditional, and only ended when Lionel was taken ill at the town of Alba in Piedmont – which was part of Visconti's dowry – where he died on 17 October 1368, allegedly from overeating.

Alba is famous for its white truffles and its wines, including Dolcetto, Barbera, and Nebbiolo. But there was speculation at the time that Lionel had been poisoned, either by his new father-in-law, Galeazzo II – who, when challenged, protested his innocence in a sworn deposition – or by Bernabò, his new wife's uncle, although this has never been proved, and both allegations may simply reflect the Viscontis' unsavoury reputation. Lionel's body was later transported back to England for burial at Clare in Suffolk, the home of his first wife. In his will, dated 3 October 1368, Lionel left his black suit and 'a piece of embroidered black cloth' to the church at Clare, and his jewels and gold-embroidered cloak to Violante. She endured two further unhappy marriages before dying in November 1386 at the age of thirty-two.

Possibly, Chaucer stayed in Italy until Lionel's death in October. In the sense that its original purpose was to cement the alliance between England and Lombardy, the trip ended in failure. But there was another aspect of the Milan visit with a more profound impact on the history of literature: if Chaucer did attend the festivities after the wedding, or perhaps even the wedding itself, he would have encountered a number of other writers who are known to have been present, including Jean Froissart – who, as we have seen, was in Lionel's party – Francesco Petrarch and possibly Giovanni Boccaccio.

The poet Froissart Chaucer would have known already: Froissart, after all, came from Valenciennes in the province of Hainault, the home of both Queen Philippa and Chaucer's wife, and was the famed author of the illuminated *Chronicles*, the best-known account of medieval chivalry and courtly ideals at the time of the Hundred Years' War, the Black Death, and the Peasants' Revolt. He served – like Chaucer himself – in the court of Edward III and Queen Philippa in London, was close to Lionel and the Black Prince, and is known to have travelled in Scotland as well as France, Spain, and Italy. He also wrote a 'rhyming chronicle' for Queen Philippa some six years before Lionel's Milan wedding.

Another wedding guest who played a significant role in Chaucer's life was John Hawkwood, the condottiere of the mercenary army known as the White Company, who at the time was in the pay of Galeazzo II Visconti and was quartered with his forces nearby at Pavia, where Galeazzo II had constructed a castle as his power base in 1360. All troops in the Middle Ages were hired for particular campaigns – there were no standing armies as such in England until the Civil War in the seventeenth century – and Hawkwood always made clear that his first loyalty as a knight was to the English Crown, regardless of which rival Italian city state he was fighting for at the time.

The Visconti–Lionel wedding may even have been Hawkwood's idea, not only bringing the Viscontis and the Plantagenets closer together but also aiming at persuading the then-pope, Urban V, that if he stopped backing England's enemies in France during the Hundred Years' War then Edward III would use his new influence in Lombardy to undermine the pope's enemies in Italy. Chaucer would have dealings with Hawkwood ten years later, in 1378.

The Milan wedding would also have provided an opportunity to encounter the masters of medieval Italian poetry: Petrarch and Boccaccio. Petrarch had taken up residence at Pavia in 1364, writing to Boccaccio that he was thoroughly enjoying the mild temperatures and occasional showers in a city built on a little hill. William Rossiter has pointed out that Petrarch – who was sixty-four at the time of the Milan wedding and had an ulcerated leg – left Milan to return to Pavia on 3 July, two weeks before Chaucer left England. On the other hand there is no reason why Chaucer could not himself have ridden to Pavia, which is only 45 km from Milan.

Milan and Pavia would have had a profound impact on the man who was about to write the *Book of the Duchess* for John of Gaunt, and who at the age of twenty-six was starting out his career as a poet as well as a diplomat and courtier: Chaucer, by his own account, wrote 'many a song and many a lecherous lay'. Whether he first met him at the Milan wedding feast or during later trips to Italy, Chaucer would have been impressed by Francesco Petrarch, who had succeeded Dante as the supreme Italian poet and was nurturing the genius of Boccaccio, to whom he wrote lyrical accounts of his time in Pavia (though Boccaccio refused to join him there because he had no time for the tyrannical Viscontis).

As Piero Boitani notes, 'Dante, Boccaccio and Petrarch

must have appeared as a striking avant-garde to the Chaucer who came to them from an essentially Anglo-French culture'. If Dante presented himself 'as both a prophet and Virgil's ideal successor,' Petrarch was 'the father of the Renaissance', was crowned on the Capitoline Hill as Italy's supreme poet, and – for Chaucer – was an example to revere and follow. The Elizabethan and Jacobean schoolmaster Thomas Speght wrote in his 1598 edition of the works of Chaucer (the '*antient and lerned English poet*') that 'some write' that Chaucer 'with Petrarke was present at the marriage of Lionell Duke of Clarence with Violant daughter of Galeasius Duke of Millaine'. The papal historian and physician Paolo Giovio had not mentioned Chaucer in his account, Speght noted, 'and yet it may well be: for it is in record that twice or thrice he was emploied in foraine countries'.

'*I wol yow telle a tale which that I lerned at Padowe of a worthy clerk, as preved by his wordes and his werk*', says the Clerk in the *Canterbury Tales*. '*He is now deed and nayled in his cheste; I prey to God so yeve his soule reste!*' This late, great writer, the Clerk tells us, was '*Fraunceys Petrak, the lauriat poete*', who had '*Enlumyned al Ytaille of poetrie*'. Or, in Peter Ackroyd's version:

I will tell you a story I first heard from a worthy scholar at the University of Padua. He was a very learned man, and a good one. Alas he is now dead and nailed in his coffin. God give him rest.

This scholar was also a great poet, Francis Petrarch by name. Have you heard of him?

3

Francesco Petrarch

Francesco Petrarch was about sixty-four at the time of the Milan wedding, while Chaucer was around twenty-six. Petrarch was nearing the end of his life, whereas Chaucer was just starting out. In fact, Chaucer's trip to Italy four years later in 1372–3 came just a year before Petrarch's death on 19 July 1374.

Petrarch by then was living in the town of Arqua in the Veneto, 25 km from Padua, where he spent the last four years of his life (from 1370 to 1374) together with his daughter, Francesca; his son-in-law, Francescuolo da Brossano; and his granddaughter, Eletta. The house at Arqua (renamed Arqua Petrarca in the nineteenth century) is the most likely place for Chaucer to have met the great Italian poet. It had been given to Petrarch by the Lord of Padua, Francesco I da Carrara, who was his patron and close friend. Now a museum dedicated to Petrarch, it is approached by cobbled roads high in the town, with a view of the pointed volcanic Euganean Hills (Colli Euganei). Surrounded by olive trees, vines and almond trees, the house is decorated with late-sixteenth-century frescoes illustrating Petrarch's works from *Africa* to the *Canzoniere*, financed by a later wealthy owner – and Petrarch enthusiast – Pietro Paolo Vandezocco from Padua. But it also contains period furniture and a library, and has a striking external staircase and loggia together with a walled garden in which Petrarch is said to have taken a keen interest. Surviving curiosities inside the house include books and manuscripts of the period and the chair on which Petrarch was sitting when he died, his head resting on a book by Virgil on his desk. There is also a glass cabinet containing his mummified cat, which has been admired over the centuries by visitors including Byron, although – like the frescoes – it probably dates from long after Petrarch's time.

The town features a fountain fed by local springs, now known as Petrarch's Fountain, as well as Petrarch's impressive tomb of red Verona marble in front of the church of Santa Maria Assunta, bearing an inscription that reads 'This stone covers the cold bones of Francesco Petrarca; receive O Virgin Mother his soul, and you, Son of the Virgin, pardon him.'

A local delicacy is *brodo di giuggiole,* a sweet liqueur made from the jujube, an exotic dark brown local fruit resembling large olives, celebrated in the Jujube Festival held in Arqua every October. Local people dress up in medieval costume for the festival, with one representing Petrarch himself, wearing the laurel wreath of the Poet Laureate. The fruit has even given rise to a phrase, *'andare in brodo di giuggiole',* meaning 'to be beside oneself with joy' or 'to be tickled pink'. Other Arqua festivals celebrate lavender and the local aromatic herbs, as well as honey from local bees, olive oil, and herbal teas. Petrarch must have been 'tickled pink' by them all in his retirement – as no doubt Chaucer would have been too.

In the *Canterbury Tales*, the Clerk – or Chaucer – quite clearly says he heard the story he is about to tell from '*Fraunceys Petrak, the lauriat poete*'. Derek Pearsall finds it unlikely that Chaucer met Petrarch at Arqua, adding that Chaucer would not in any case have been well received because Petrarch was by then 'old and crotchety, and very distinguished, and did not have time for young travellers of no rank'. William Rossiter notes that there is no record in Petrarch's voluminous correspondence of such a meeting: 'A surprise visit from a young English poet would certainly have merited at least a couple of lines in a letter.'

On the other hand, although Petrarch was certainly 'crotchety', Rossiter adds, 'there is no reason to believe that he would have turned away a visitor on account of the latter's being "of no rank"'. The Italian scholar Cino Chiarini, who published a translation of some of the *Canterbury Tales* into Italian at the end of the nineteenth century, and who in 1902 analysed Chaucer's reliance on Dante for his *House of Fame,* was convinced that Chaucer and Petrarch had met, and that neither age nor social rank would have been an obstacle.

Like Chaucer, Petrarch was not himself of noble birth: he had been born in 1304 in a substantial but middle-class house in Arezzo in Tuscany, at 28 Via dell'Orto. Now the Petrarch House Museum, with a collection of books and paintings, it was rebuilt in the sixteenth century and restored in the 1920s, but some of the earlier house survives, notably the ground floor, where Petrarch is said to have been born. A monumental marble statue of him surrounded by figures drawn from his works was erected in 1928 on the orders of King Victor Emmanuel III in the nearby Il Prato Park.

Petrarch was the son of Ser Petracco, a lawyer, and his wife, Eletta Canigiani: his given name was Francesco Petracco, later Latinised to Petrarca, which became anglicised as Petrarch. He clearly had a good start in life, given that his father was a well-to-do notary, a figure of some prominence in Arezzo who knew Dante Alighieri and counted the great poet as a friend until the latter's death in Ravenna in 1321. The 700th anniversary of Dante's death was widely celebrated in Italy – and in Britain – in 2021.

Petrarch was only seventeen at the time of Dante's death, but he never forgot his illustrious predecessor. Suggestions that he was jealous of Dante or even held him in contempt, Petrarch declared in a letter to Boccaccio, were 'an odious and ridiculous invention'. In reality, he appreciated Dante's genius; his mastery of vernacular Italian; the 'noble beauty' of his style, which was 'the best of its kind'; and his 'friendship with my father'.

Ser Petracco had been clerk of one of the courts in Florence, but he was banished from Florence as a member of the White Guelphs in 1302, two years before Petrarch's birth. The Guelphs had backed the pope against the Ghibellines, supporters of the Holy Roman Emperor, but then in a bout of typical political infighting they split into two rival factions, White and Black, with the Black Guelphs loyal to the unscrupulous Pope Boniface VIII despite his role in manipulating the resignation and imprisonment of his predecessor, the mild-mannered and reluctant pontiff Pope Celestine V.

The Black Guelphs controlled Florence, unfortunately for Petrarch's father, and indeed for Dante, who was also a White Guelph, and who was also exiled.

When Petrarch was still a child, his family moved again – not exactly back to Florence but close, this time to the village of Incisa, in the Val d'Arno, some 20 km from Florence, where Petrarch's younger brother Gherardo was born in 1307. But when in 1309 the French-born Pope Clement V decided to move the papacy from Rome to Avignon in France, Petrarch's parents decided that they too would move to Avignon to support the new pope.

Petrarch's father insisted that Francesco and his brother both study law, which Petrarch dutifully did, first at the University of Montpellier from 1316 to 1320, and then at Bologna from 1320 to 1323. But he found the legal system shot through with manipulation and corruption. He decided he was not meant to be a lawyer at all but instead was a born writer with 'an unquenchable thirst for literature', as he put it in a letter. His father disagreed: despite his friendship with Dante, he thought books were a distraction for the young Petrarch and even threw some of them into the fire (though he is said to have relented by retrieving copies of Virgil and Cicero). When Ser Petracco died in 1326, Petrarch returned to Avignon and spent most of his time writing, starting with *Africa*, a lengthy poem in Latin about the great Roman general Scipio Africanus. He took minor orders in the service of Cardinal Giovanni Colonna, but this was a light religious duty that only bound him to the daily reading of his office.

Africa was just the beginning: Petrarch travelled widely

in Europe; arguably invented tourism by climbing up Mont Ventoux to admire the views; collected manuscripts to preserve the works of Greek writers such as Homer and Roman writers such as Cicero and Livy; and, in 1345, discovered a collection of Cicero's letters not previously known to have existed, the collection *Epistulae ad Atticum*, in the Biblioteca Capitolare of Verona Cathedral. And he wrote poetry. On 8 April 1341, Petrarch was crowned Poet Laureate by two Roman senators, Giordano Orsini and Orso dell'Anguillara, on Rome's Capitoline Hill.

Petrarch is credited – or charged, depending on your point of view – with having coined the term 'Dark Ages' to describe the years following the fall of the Roman Empire in the West. He admired not only Dante as a pioneer of enlightenment after a period of cultural darkness but also Giotto, whose frescoes he described as having a beauty that 'amazes the masters of art', adding, 'although the ignorant cannot understand it'. When the plague struck Italy in 1348, Petrarch said it 'left us alone and forlorn ... these losses are irreparable', but his faith in human creativity was not shaken.

Petrarch was a prolific letter writer, not least to his friend and fellow writer Boccaccio. He is considered 'the father of humanism', even the 'father of the Renaissance': he saw no contradiction between his Christian faith and the study of human thought – including Greek and Roman traditions – or the development of secular creativity and achievement.

He did most of his writing in Latin – poems, scholarly works, essays, even letters. John Larner has suggested that if Chaucer did meet Petrarch at the Milan wedding in 1368, he would have been subjected to 'a discourse on the vanity of vernacular literature'. Petrarch's *Secretum meum* ('my secret book') is an imaginary dialogue with a figure inspired by Augustine of Hippo; his *Remedies for Fortune Fair and Foul* is a self-help book that was popular for hundreds of years; *Itinerarium* is his 'guide to the Holy Land'; and *Bucolicum carmen* is a collection of twelve pastoral poems.

Despite his attachment to Latin, Petrarch is best remembered today for the poetry he wrote in Italian, notably *Fragments of Vernacular Matters*; the *Triumphi* ('triumphs'), a six-part narrative poem inspired by Dante; and a collection of 366 lyric poems or sonnets better known as the *Canzoniere* ('songbook'), in which he famously celebrates his love for a woman called Laura, whom he first saw in the church of Sainte-Claire at Avignon on Good Friday, 6 April 1327, when he was twenty-two. One theory is that, despite this supposed encounter in Avignon, Laura did not actually exist and was an invention of his youthful imagination (which Petrarch always denied); another, however, is that she certainly did exist and was Laura de Noves, the wife of Count Hugues de Sade, an ancestor of the Marquis de Sade. Petrarch describes her as fair-haired, modest, dignified, and – of course – very attractive. Laura and Petrarch had little or no personal contact, however: as he wrote in *Secretum meum*, she refused him because she was already married.

Instead, he began a stream of love poems. His frequent use in them of the word *l'aura* is a clear reference not only to Laura but also to the spiritual or ethereal atmosphere he experienced when seeing the object of his hopeless ardour: among the most famous is Sonnet 90, which describes Laura as 'a celestial spirit, a living sun' with an 'angelic form', among other accolades:

> *Erano i capei d'oro a l'aura sparsi*
> *che 'n mille dolci nodi gli avolgea,*
> *e 'l vago lume oltra misura ardea*
> *di quei begli occhi, ch'or ne son sì scarsi;*
>
> *e 'l viso di pietosi color' farsi,*
> *non so se vero o falso, mi parea:*
> *i' che l'esca amorosa al petto avea,*
> *qual meraviglia se di sùbito arsi?*

She let her gold hair scatter in the breeze
that twined it in a thousand sweet knots,
and wavering light, beyond measure, would burn
in those beautiful eyes, which are now so dim:

and it seemed to me her face wore the colour
of pity, I do not know whether false or true:
I who had the lure of love in my breast,
what wonder if I suddenly caught fire?

It is thought that Laura was the reason Petrarch bought a small estate near Avignon in 1337. When she died in 1348, Petrarch – by now forty-four – found his grief was as difficult to live with as his former despair and anguish over not being able to form a relationship with her. In his *Letter to Posterity*, Petrarch writes:

In my younger days I struggled constantly with an overwhelming but pure love affair – my only one, and I would have struggled with it longer had not premature death, bitter but salutary for me, extinguished the cooling flames. I certainly wish I could say that I have always been entirely free from desires of the flesh, but I would be lying if I did.

Some suggest that Petrarch's account of his ascent of Mont Ventoux (1,909 m), not far from Carpentras in Vaucluse, was – like his relationship with Laura – exaggerated, possibly even fictional. Petrarch tells us that on 26 April 1336, with his brother and two servants, he walked to the top of Mont Ventoux, and that he did so both for exercise and for the breathtaking views. Petrarch described the feat in a letter to his confessor, the monk Dionigi di Borgo San Sepolcro, claiming he had taken inspiration from Philip V of Macedonia (reigned 221–179 BC), who reportedly climbed Mount Haemo in the Balkan Mountains (now part of Bulgaria). Petrarch said he was also galvanised into action by an aged shepherd or herdsman who told him he had climbed Mont Ventoux (also known as the Giant of Provence) some fifty years before and had suffered broken bones and torn clothes, claimed that nobody had climbed it since, and warned Petrarch not to even try.

There may indeed have been some exaggeration in Petrarch's account: the French philosopher Jean Buridan had climbed the same mountain a few years earlier on his way to the papal court at Avignon, and other ascents accomplished during the Middle Ages have been recorded, including by Anno II, the eleventh-century archbishop of Cologne and regent of the Holy Roman Empire. It is now part of the Tour de France bicycle race. None the less, Petrarch's letter to Dionigi is seen as an early example of the glories of mountaineering, coupled with dedication to Christian values: Petrarch tells us that when he reached the summit he took from his pocket Saint Augustine's *Confessions*, which he always carried with him, and read the words, 'Men wonder at the heights of the mountains and the mighty waves of the sea, the wide sweep of rivers and the circuit of the ocean, and the revolution of the stars, but themselves they consider not'. He tells us:

> I closed the book, angry with myself that I should still
> be admiring earthly things who might long ago have
> learned from even the pagan philosophers that nothing is
> wonderful but the soul, which, great itself, finds nothing
> great outside itself. Then, in truth, I was satisfied that I
> had seen enough of the mountain; I turned my inward
> eye upon myself, and from that time not a syllable fell
> from my lips until we reached the bottom again … We
> look about us for what is to be found only within …
> How many times, think you, did I turn back that day,
> to glance at the summit of the mountain which seemed
> scarcely a cubit high compared with the range of human
> contemplation?

In the 1350s, Petrarch moved from France back to Italy, first to Milan in the service of the Viscontis, despite criticism that they were the enemies of Florence, and then to Padua.

Petrarch could not marry because of his church career as a canon at Monselice near Padua, but is none the less said to have fathered two children: a son, Giovanni, who was born in 1337 and died of the plague in 1361, and a daughter, Francesca, born in 1343. Francesca and her family came to live with Petrarch at the Palazzo Molina in Venice and, as we have seen, in 1368 they all returned together to the Padua area, to Arqua, where Petrarch died just before his seventieth birthday.

Petrarch's will (dated 4 April 1370) left fifty florins to his writer friend Boccaccio 'to buy a warm winter dressing gown'; various legacies (a horse, a silver cup, a lute, and a Madonna) to his brother and his friends; his house in Vaucluse to its caretaker; and the bulk of his estate to his son-in-law, Francescuolo da Brossano, who was to give half of it to 'the person to whom, as he knows, I wish it to go' – presumably meaning his daughter, Francesca, da Brossano's wife. There is no mention in the will of Petrarch's famous library, which he had promised to the city of Venice in exchange for the Palazzo Molina. This arrangement was probably annulled when he moved to Padua, Venice's arch-rival, in 1368. The library was later seized by the Padua authorities, and his books and manuscripts were dispersed. Petrarch's reputation as a founder of Italian literature, however, was enhanced by the powerful Venetian cardinal Pietro Bembo, who was himself a poet and published an edition of Petrarch's verse in 1501 during the Renaissance (which Petrarch was said to have inspired, or even invented).

In November 2003, it was announced that Petrarch's body would be exhumed from its sarcophagus in Arqua Petrarca. A team of experts from Padua University planned to reconstruct his cranium and recreate his features digitally to mark the 700th anniversary of his birth. They also aimed to verify reports that he was 1.83 m (about six feet) tall, an usually large height for the time. But this wasn't the first time Petrarch's resting place had been disturbed. In 1873, Professor Giovanni Canestrini, also of Padua University, had investigated the remains. But in 2003, the researchers reopened the tomb only to find the skull in pieces and a DNA test proved that in any case it was not Petrarch's skull at all. The researchers concluded, however, that the rest of the skeleton in the tomb was indeed Petrarch's, since it was not only as tall as reported but also appeared to match injuries Petrarch described in his writings, including an injury sustained when he was kicked by a donkey at the age of forty-two.

4

The Tale of Patient Griselda

What Chaucer took from Petrarch – by his own account – was not his devotion to Laura, or his love of mountaineering, but his version of the story of Griselda. This tells of a woman who endures appalling suffering and humiliation at the hands of a husband who tests her obedience and loyalty to the limit and beyond. 'The Clerk's Tale' is Chaucer's version of the narrative – but is it based on the final story in Boccaccio's *Decameron* or on Petrarch's later elegant Latin adaptation?

The story – to take Petrarch's version as an example, though all three follow the same narrative – takes place in Saluzzo (now in Cuneo Province in Piedmont), at the foot of 'the very lofty' Monte Viso in the Cottian Alps, the source of the River Po, the 'king of rivers', 'which rises from a small spring on the mountain's side' and eventually empties into the Adriatic. Walter, the greatest of the 'noble marquises' ruling the area, is clearly 'marked out for leadership', except that he has no thought for the future – and shrinks 'from even a hint of marriage', on the grounds that he values 'complete liberty'.

His subjects, however, anxious about the lack of an heir, persuade Walter to marry, and he chooses Grisildis (Griselda), a girl from a poor background who tends her father's sheep and is remarkable for 'the beauty of her character and spirit as well as her body'. Walter, we are told, had often 'cast his eyes on this little maid, not with lust but with the sober thoughts of an older man', and – to the astonishment of the people, her father, and the girl herself – he asks for her hand, offering 'golden rings, coronets and girdles', which everyone had assumed were for a woman of noble birth.

Griselda duly shows her 'remarkable virtue', maturity, and wisdom as Walter's wife, and gives birth to a baby daughter. But the obsessive, unhinged Walter, seized with 'a desire more strange than laudable', decides to test her obedience by telling her he intends to have the little girl killed. Griselda replies that Walter is her master and can do as he wishes, only telling the servant who is sent to take her daughter not to let 'beasts or birds tear her little body'. She makes the sign of the cross and lets her daughter go.

Instead of having the girl murdered, however, Walter has his daughter taken secretly to Bologna to be brought up by his sister. Four years later, Griselda again gives birth, this time to a son, and once again Walter tells her the child is to be killed, while again secretly having him taken to Bologna. When the missing daughter turns twelve, Walter pretends the pope has agreed to annul his marriage to Griselda and has the daughter brought back from Bologna to be his new wife, telling Griselda she must give up her dowry and fine clothes and jewels and return to her former humble home, adding spitefully, 'No good fortune lasts forever.'

The patient Griselda wishes him well with his new bride

and keeps only her shift, saying, 'Naked I came from my father's house and naked I shall return.' Before her daughter arrives, together with her son, now seven, Griselda is put to work cleaning Walter's house, making the beds, and setting the tables 'like the best of handmaids'. She then greets her daughter – not recognising her – and the other guests 'with cheerful face and marvellous sweetness' until Walter, 'able to bear it no longer', tells her that these are her own children and that she has proved her fidelity, adding, 'nor do I think that under heaven there is another woman who has undergone such trials of her conjugal love'.

He embraces Griselda, who stands in a stupor 'as if waking from a troubled sleep', and tells her she is his 'only wife' and always will be. He justifies his appalling behaviour by saying he is 'curious and given to experiments' but 'not impious. I have tested my wife, not condemned her; I have hidden my children, not destroyed them'. Griselda, 'out of her wits' with joy and maternal love, covers her children with tears and kisses, is reclothed in fine robes and jewels, and lives in 'great peace and concord' with Walter, who moves Griselda's old father from his hovel into the palace, arranges a 'noble and honourable' marriage for his daughter, and declares his son to be his heir. He is 'happy in his wife and in his offspring'.

To modern sensibilities, what Petrarch called 'a tale of wifely obedience and faith' is a truly gruesome assertion of heartless male misogyny, coercion, and cruelty. Petrarch wrote to Boccaccio: 'My purpose in rewriting your tale was not to induce the women of our time to imitate the patience of this wife, which seems to me almost beyond imitation, but to lead my readers to emulate the example of feminine constancy and submit themselves to God with the same courage as did this woman to her husband'. He had found the story by chance: Boccaccio's *Decameron*, 'written in our mother tongue and published I presume during your early years', had fallen into his hands 'I know not whence or how'.

Petrarch had not read the whole of the *Decameron*, he wrote rather archly, because it was a 'very big volume, written in prose and for the multitude', and he had more serious business to deal with and was 'much pressed for time'. But he had given the book a hasty perusal, 'running through it like a traveller', and, as was usual when looking through a book in a hurry, he 'read more carefully at the beginning and at the end'. Boccaccio's sense of humour he found 'a little too free at times', but that was excusable given 'the age at which you wrote, the style and language you employ, and the frivolity of the subjects and of the persons likely to read such tales'.

Moreover, Boccaccio had begun the *Decameron* by describing accurately – and 'lamenting eloquently' – the state of Italy during the pestilence that had formed 'so dark and melancholy a period in our century'. The point, however, was that the last story, the tale of Griselda, was 'entirely different from most that precede it'. It had so struck and fascinated Petrarch that he had been 'seized with a desire to learn it by heart', and had recounted it to an audience with great effect. He had then decided to write his own version, despite being distracted and 'discontented with myself and my surroundings' – 'I suddenly sent everything flying, and snatching my pen I attacked this story of yours.' He hoped Boccaccio would be gratified even though he, Petrarch, had told the tale in Latin rather than Italian, 'in some places changing or even adding a few words, for I felt you would not only permit such alterations but would approve of them'.

He had given the result to 'one of our mutual friends in Padua', who had burst into tears and was unable to finish it, whereas another mutual friend at Verona ('for all is common between us, even our friends') had shown no emotion at all, on the grounds that although the story aroused pity it was 'all an invention' and the extraordinary patience, devotion, and constancy shown by Griselda simply did not exist. Petrarch had not replied to this friend, he said, in order to avoid turning a good-humoured discussion into a 'bitter debate'. But his private response was that 'there are some who think that whatever is difficult for them must be impossible for others', whereas there were many examples of heroic behaviour by women such as Portia (the wife of Brutus) and Alcestis (the princess in the Greek drama by Euripides), who faced death and who were therefore, Petrarch felt, 'capable of encountering any trial or form of suffering'.

Petrarch's tone is typically lofty, but his point about Griselda being an odd choice for the last story in the *Decameron* is a good one. Petrarch approves, finding the change of tone 'charming': the end of a book, he suggests, is 'where according to the principles of rhetoric the most effective part of the composition belongs'. In Boccaccio's original, the tale comes after ninety-nine other stories, most of which are light-hearted or bawdy and clearly designed to cheer up the self-isolating group at the villa during the time of plague.

Boccaccio, on the other hand, has quite a different take on the tale, which in his version is told by Dioneo, one of the three young men in the party escaping from the plague, who – clearly aware that there are seven young women in his audience, outnumbering the young men – remarks before even beginning his tale that what is done in it by Walter (Gualtieri), the Marquis of Saluzzo, is 'not an act of magnificence but an act of monstrous idiocy', adding, 'although it brought him good in the end, I don't advise anyone to imitate his actions. In fact it was a crying shame that he got good results from what he did'.

Boccaccio's version ends with Walter telling his patient wife, Griselda, that 'those who have thought me cruel and unjust and brutish' should realise 'that what I have done I did for a pre-ordained purpose', namely to 'teach you to be a wife'. At the same time, he intended to prove to himself that despite his reluctance to marry at all, he had done the right thing in choosing her. Well, says the narrator, who but Griselda could have endured the 'barbarous and unheard of tests' carried out by Walter?

Dioneo adds that 'it would probably have served him right if he happened on a wife who, once he turned her out of doors in her shift, would have found some other fellow to scrub up her fur and give her a nice new dress'. Boccaccio ends ambiguously, however, by having the ladies in the audience argue about the moral of the story 'for a long time, some inclining to one side of the story and some to the other'.

Chaucer was, of course, writing his version of the story much later, and he could have used either Petrarch's or

Boccaccio's version – or indeed both. In the *Canterbury Tales*, the story of 'Patient Griselda' is told by the Clerk, an unworldly scholar from the University of Oxford whose coat, we are told, is as 'threadbare as his purse' and who would much rather have a collection of books by Aristotle than fine clothes or musical instruments.

In 'The Clerk's Tale', Griselda is seen – as she is by both Petrarch and Boccaccio – as someone who endures all trials because they are God's will. God, the Clerk says, knows all human frailties, since he created them in the first place, but does everything 'for our own good' and, as St James said, 'will never tempt us beyond our strength'. The story follows familiar lines, though with typical Chaucerian additions and interjections by the Clerk: Griselda's father is a poor labourer, but then 'was not the Son of God born in a simple stable?' But, like Boccaccio rather than Petrarch, Chaucer's Clerk clearly blames Walter for causing his wife – an innocent victim – 'anguish and dread'. He remarks at one point, 'There was no need for any of this, but men can become ruthless when they are married to patient and pliable wives.' Walter, in Chaucer's version, comes to be regarded by the people as a 'wicked man' who, it was thought, had had his children killed 'for the crime of being born to a wife of lowly estate ... Who does not detest and despise a murderer?' The Clerk is scathing, too, about public opinion: people are as fickle and unstable as a weathervane; they wax and wane like the moon; their opinions are worthless; only a fool would believe anything they say. 'Male clerks are all too ready to honour the achievements of other men,' the Clerk says. 'They rarely mention women but, in

truth, women are far more faithful and patient than any man.'
Women, he adds, are kinder and more trustworthy than men,
'then and now', and 'if someone has a different opinion, I will
be astonished'.

The Clerk – or Chaucer – insists that it was Petrarch who
told him this story at Padua, explaining 'that he had composed
it in a high style fitting its matter'. Petrarch, we are told, had
described to the Clerk (or Chaucer) the area around Saluzzo
and the Apennines on the western border of Lombardy, and
in particular Monte Viso, the highest of the mountains and
the source of the River Po 'in a little spring among the rocks',
from which the river ran east, 'increasing all the way' through
Ferrara and Venetia before entering the sea. The Clerk even
quotes Petrarch directly at the end of the story, noting that
Petrarch claimed he had not told it in order to advise women
to be submissive: 'They could not, and should not, copy the
patience of Griselda. The real lesson is more simple. Every
man and woman should, like her, try to be steadfast in adver-
sity. That is enough.' That, Chaucer adds, 'is why Petrarch
chose to narrate the story of Griselda in his most noble prose',
meaning in formal Latin rather than everyday Italian.

The Clerk does allow himself a note of misogyny, telling the
'lords and ladies of the pilgrimage' that there is no Griselda
to be found in England, where 'if you put a wife or mother to
the test, you would find more brass than gold'. But on the
whole his version is in fact much closer to Boccaccio's, with
its scathing condemnation of Walter's 'barbarous' behaviour
and 'monstrous idiocy', than it is to Petrarch's. 'Griselda is
dead and lies buried somewhere in the land of Italy,' the Clerk

concludes. 'Her patience was rewarded in the end. But I beg all you husbands never to test your wives as Walter tested her. Your efforts will not work. You will fail.' As for wives, they must 'never let humility nail down your tongue … Don't allow men to get the better of you'. Far from fearing their husbands, wives should make them jealous, frighten them by accusing them of something, and 'if you are good-looking, make use of it. Show off your features, and your dress. If you are ugly, spend your money freely and make friends with everyone … Let your husband do the wailing and lamenting. That is all I have to say'.

It is a conclusion closer not only to Boccaccio but also to the views of Chaucer's own plain-speaking and much-married Wife of Bath. In the *Canterbury Tales*, she tells the story of a knight at the time of King Arthur who eventually concedes that it is women who control a marriage, and she concludes, 'God send us all gentle husbands – especially if they are young and good in bed … Cursed be the men who will not obey their wives.'

'Naturally I have nothing against the Wife of Bath,' the Clerk says as he finishes his version of the Griselda story. 'May God give her, and those like her, a good life! Long may she rule over us!' Chaucer – as we shall see – never mentions Boccaccio, as opposed to Petrarch. But on the basis of the evidence it seems hard not to conclude that he drew on the work of both – including the story of Patient Griselda – and he certainly had the opportunity to meet both writers during his visits to Italy.

In 'The Wife of Bath's Tale', in complete contrast to the

image of passive women in the story of Griselda, a knight is told he can avoid being executed for a rape if he answers the age-old riddle 'What do women want?', a question later asked by Freud (and in our own time by Nancy Meyers' 2000 film *What Women Want*, starring Mel Gibson). In Chaucer, the question is '*What thyng is it that wommen moost desiren?*' To find that out, the knight finally consults an 'old crone', who tells him the answer is simply that women want their own way in life – and who turns into a young and beautiful woman when he accepts her answer.

There is no direct counterpart to 'The Wife of Bath's Tale' in the *Decameron* – but there is a passage in Boccaccio that could have inspired the Wife of Bath's spirited assertions of independence, namely the prologue to the sixth day. In this, the 'bossy' maid, Licisca, tells the assembled company – in a positively Chaucerian outburst – that all women play tricks on their husbands to get their own way and are cleverer than men at concealing their love affairs, adding, 'I haven't a single female friend who went to her husband as a virgin'.

John Finlayson has noted, 'It used to be thought that Chaucer did not use Boccaccio's *Decameron* as a source for any of the *Canterbury Tales*, and indeed was unaware of that work's existence.' Indeed, there were a number of French versions drawn from Boccaccio, with which Chaucer may have been familiar. However, as Helen Cooper remarks in *The Structure of the Canterbury Tales*, it 'strains credibility' to believe that the circumstantial evidence for Chaucer's knowledge of the *Decameron* is 'mere coincidence', let alone 'that he found the inspiration for the *Canterbury Tales* in Boccaccio's uninspired imitators'. Chaucer's version may be from Petrarch, Finlay-son concludes, but is undoubtedly 'derived directly from the *Decameron,* though of course with innumerable small but significant additions and verbal felicities which make the Tale a typical Chaucerian production'.

Chaucer's source for 'The Clerk's Tale' was undoubtedly Petrarch's version of the Griselda story, as the Clerk says. But Petrarch himself acknowledges in his preface that he took the story from Boccaccio, and, quite apart from the tone of disgust over Walter's behaviour, there are elements in Chaucer's version that are in Boccaccio but not in Petrarch – for example, Griselda's vow of obedience to Walter when she agrees to marry him. Whereas Petrarch is neutral about Griselda's fate, Boccaccio and Chaucer both sympathise with her: Boccaccio ends with the thought that only Griselda could have endured the 'cruel and unheard of trials' imposed on her by Walter, adding, 'What more needs to be said, except that celestial spirits may sometimes descend even into the houses of the poor, whilst there are those in royal palaces who would be better employed as swineherds than as rulers of men?' In Boccaccio, the Marquis is guilty of '*matta bestialitade*', mad bestiality or inhuman wickedness, a damning phrase taken from Dante's *Inferno.*

Quite possibly, Chaucer found Boccaccio more democratic and down to earth than the rather elitist Petrarch. He would have come across the *Decameron,* and possibly Boccaccio himself, in Boccaccio's home town, Florence, which Chaucer visited in 1373. But his journeys took him first to another key Italian city state: Genoa.

5

A Mission to Genoa

Four years after the royal marriage in Milan, Chaucer found himself drawn back to matters Italian. Chaucer was absent from England for six months, travelling to Genoa and Florence from 1 December 1372 until 23 May 1373; the reason for his journey this time was a combination of trade and royal diplomacy. 'Galfridus Chaucer', 'scutifer [squire] domini regis', was commissioned to head to Genoa with two Genoese officials in London: Jacopo (Jacob, or James) di Provano (an anglicisation of the Italian Provana), who was originally from a noble family at Carignano on the River Po near Turin in Piedmont, and Giovanni (John) di Mari, who was from a leading Genoese family prominent in the Church, the military, and trade.

Both Italians were in the king's service in London, and Chaucer accompanied them on 'secret business' concerning English trade with Genoa, on the Ligurian coast. The Provano family were bankers to Edward III; importantly for our story, the Genoa trip would have given Chaucer the opportunity to stay as a guest at Carignano, which is just over 30 km from Saluzzo, the setting for the story of Patient Griselda (including in Chaucer's version, 'The Clerk's Tale'). Other members of the Provano family may also have been involved in the trip: Peter and Hugh Provan are described in English court documents as being 'among the king's bankers' and 'merchants of the bishopric of Turin'.

The mission to Genoa and Florence apparently also included Jacopo di Provano's son, Saladin – an odd choice of name at first sight, given that Saladin was the victorious leader of the Muslim resistance to the Crusaders. On the other hand, Saladin, who defeated Crusader forces at Jerusalem, Acre, and the Horns of Hattin above the Sea of Galilee, was none the less widely respected in the West as a 'chivalrous knight' who had granted an amnesty to defeated Christian troops (provided they paid a ransom), and he was favourably depicted in Boccaccio's *Decameron*.

The other Genoese official, Giovanni di Mari – also variously referred to in the records as 'del Mare', 'de Mare' and 'Jean de Mari' – was evidently quite an operator, supplying Edward III not only with Genoese mercenaries but also with jewellery and imported luxury goods. In February 1359, over a decade before the Genoa expedition, he is recorded as having 'brought to England for the king's use crowns, chapulets (*circulos*) [a chapulet or chaplet was a wreath of beads and flowers worn on the head], gold rings, precious stones and jewels, many of which the king has bought'. Edward decreed that di Mari did not have to pay duty on these items, whether they were brought to England 'for the king's use or his own', provided that he paid 'custom and subsidy' on all his other 'goods and merchandise'. An entry for May 1358 even described di

Mari as 'the king's merchant' and offered him royal protection, recording 'the affection which the king bears to him for
his merits, as for useful services to the king daily done by him'.
In January 1361, di Mari sent 'some yeomen and servants of
his with goods and merchandise to Genoa to further special
business of the king', and was given safe conduct for his ship,
the *Rede Cogge* ('red cog' – a cog, usually made of oak, was a
ship with a single mast and sail) for a year.

In February 1367, one of di Mari's vessels transporting
wool, cloth, linen, curtains, 'and other merchandise' from
Flanders was shipwrecked at Plymouth, and – inevitably –
the cargo was looted. Di Mari complained that although the
local mayors and bailiffs had been charged to find out 'into
whose hands those goods came', and apparently did find
'divers goods', they had failed to return them, to the 'hurt
and impoverishment' of the 'alien merchants' such as himself
'who by bringing their goods into the realm brought 'great
advantage to the king and all his people'.

The Genoese, in other words, were firmly established at the
heart of English trade – and state. In February 1373, a certain
Francis di Mari, possibly the son of Giovanni di Mari, was
described as 'captain and leader of the Genoese crossbowmen
engaged for the king's service'. They were evidently a quarrel-
some lot, since Francis was given 'full power' by the king to
'appease and pacify the debates and dissensions which, as the
king is informed, often break out among them' and to 'chastise
by imprisonment or otherwise any refusing to be brought to
justice'. But squabbles apart, the *balestrieri genovese* ('Genoese
crossbowmen') who were recruited not only from Genoa but

from across Liguria, had been a formidable force since the First Crusade in the eleventh century, and had fought for the French at the Battle of Crecy in 1346.

Chaucer therefore knew some of Genoa's most prominent merchants and officials before he even set foot in Liguria – and was travelling with two men, di Mari and di Provano, who were a key part of court life in London. A royal decree of 12 November 1372 empowered Chaucer, di Provano, and di Mari to 'treat with Dominicus [di] Campofregoso, Duke of Genoa, concerning the grant of a place on the English coast for Genoese merchants'. Chaucer was given 100 marks 'to treat with the Genoese' concerning this appointment of a special seaport in England for the use of Genoese merchants, despite opposition from traders in London. As Andrew Galloway has noted, 'In 1372–3 Chaucer was sent by the aged king or his advisers on a mission to Genoa to negotiate a dedicated English port for the Genoese traders – a goal that the English crown and Genoese merchants desired but most London merchants detested.'

The Genoese already had an English port that they regularly used: Southampton. As we have seen, Chaucer spent some of his boyhood there, after his father was made deputy butler to the king at Southampton, so must have encountered the Genoese merchants at close quarters. The Genoese, the Florentines, and the Venetians all had fleets of galleys that traded in alum, dyes, silk, spices, carpets, and even parrots and monkeys between Flanders and Southampton, with the ships taking much-prized English wool – especially from the Cotswolds – back to the Continent. Italian communities were established at the port, with traders marrying local women and worshipping at Southampton's churches, the Genoese favouring the Franciscan Friary in the High Street (sadly long gone, another victim of the Dissolution under Henry VIII). The Italians took over much of Bugle Street, near Southampton's harbour, now much modernised, although the splendid Merchant's House in nearby French Street (managed by English Heritage) still survives to give an impression of how they lived.

The links between England and Genoa were not confined to trade and diplomacy, however – they shared mutual military interests, in particular naval power. On 22 November, just ten days after the announcement of Chaucer's royal mission, Pietro (Peter) di Campofregoso, brother of the Duke – or Doge – of Genoa, was appointed captain of King Edward's galleys – in other words, admiral of the English fleet. Jacopo di Provano was his deputy. Such appointments were normally short term, and Campofregoso may not even have taken up the post in any case, given that he was asked by Genoa to lead the capture of Famagusta and invasion of Cyprus in October the same year. None the less, the move to give a Genoese noble such a key naval command was remarkable given that hitherto the Genoese had been on the side of the French rather than the English in the Hundred Years' War, and it proves that Edward III wanted the Genoese not only to provide England with its mercenaries in future but also to help develop an English navy. Di Provano was a key figure in this enterprise: he was given the huge sum of nearly 10,000 pounds to hire war galleys from Genoa and was promised up to ten ships for the summer of 1372 – though as far as we know they never materialised.

At the time of the Battle of Sluys, one of the opening confrontations with France in 1340, at a port between Zeeland and Flanders, Edward did not have a permanent navy as such: the English fleet assembled 150 ships against France's 230, but they were almost all merchant ships commandeered at short notice into military service. The French ships, despite being backed by Genoese mercenary forces, lost Sluys when bad weather disrupted their formation and the French vessels became entangled with each other, allowing the English to attack, with huge French losses. But by June 1372 – just six months before Chaucer's Genoese mission – the English fleet was proving not so lucky. Despite being three times larger, it lost disastrously to a joint force of French and Spanish (Castilian) warships at the Battle of La Rochelle under the command of Ambrosio Boccanegra, whose family had in 1339 provided the first Doge of Genoa: Ambrogio's uncle, Simone Boccanegra, later the subject of Giuseppe Verdi's famous opera, *Simon Boccanegra*.

The disaster at La Rochelle – recorded by Jean Froissart – cost England its naval supremacy in the Channel, and it evidently persuaded Edward III that it was time for an about-face alliance with Genoa, not least in naval matters. Chaucer, however, was walking not only into the intricacies of English–Genoese naval and military relations but also into a complex power struggle in Genoa itself: Simone Boccanegra had been deposed in 1344 and fled to safety in Pisa, only to return to office in 1356, thanks to support from the powerful Visconti family, the rulers of Milan.

Genoa was also still dealing with the aftermath of the Black Death, for which it had been a conduit thanks to its trade with the East – including the slave trade. But Genoa – like Venice and Pisa – was a major independent sea power in the Middle Ages, with an impressive harbour. Its trade with Africa and the Middle East could not be ignored, nor could its opening of Atlantic trade routes through Gibraltar. The Genoese had established power bases in Constantinople and at Caffa (now Feodosia) on the Black Sea, dealing in silk, spices, fur, and wine.

Closer to home, Genoese ships played a key role in the wool trade. English wool exports were supposed to go from Southampton to Calais, the English-owned 'staple port' at which wool was checked for quality and through which (in theory) all wool exports had to pass. But many Genoese merchants bypassed Calais, and some in Edward III's court – notably John of Gaunt, Chaucer's patron – favoured allowing the Genoese exceptional trade privileges.

Today, Chaucer would no longer recognise the harbour at Genoa, with its cruise ships and container port. But Genoa – known as 'la Superba' – still has its walled historic centre on the hill that rises above that port. The Christopher Columbus House – the childhood home of the explorer, who is said to have been born in Genoa – is an eighteenth-century reconstruction, and the great palazzi of the Strade Nuove ('new streets') built by the Genoese aristocracy date mostly from the sixteenth century, as do the bell tower and dome of the Cathedral of San Lorenzo. But much of the cathedral, including its facade and colonnades, remains as it was when it was built between the twelfth and fourteenth centuries. The cathedral's treasures include a green glass goblet said to have been brought back by Genoese Crusaders, who claimed it to be the Holy Grail used by Christ to serve wine during the Last Supper. Another symbol of medieval Genoa is the Palazzo San Giorgio, once the prison where Marco Polo wrote his *Travels* and later the headquarters of the powerful Bank of St George.

The patron saint of Genoa was John the Baptist, whose ashes were said to have been transported to Genoa in the twelfth century, and Genoa's maritime power gave it colonies from the Crimea to North Africa. Surviving symbols of Genoese expansion to the Levant can still be seen today: the Galata Tower in Istanbul, for example, or the Cembalo and Soldaia (now Sudak) fortresses in the Crimea. England even owes the flag of St George – a red cross on a white background – to Genoa, which also adopted St George as a patron saint in the Middle Ages. Genoese ships protected and transported English troops during the Crusades, and as a gesture of thanks Richard the Lionheart is said to have adopted the flag – which flew on Genoese ships – during the Third Crusade in the twelfth century. Genoa even has a claim to have invented denim cloth or fustian (the word 'jeans' derives from *Gênes*, the French name for Genoa), originally used by its sailors to cover goods on the docks and aboard ship.

The Genoese whom Chaucer dealt with, such as the *cavaliere* (knight) di Provano and his son, Saladin; di Mari, the 'king's merchant'; and Antonio d'Oria, whose Crusader ancestors had fought alongside Richard the Lionheart at Acre, all enjoyed much higher social status than either the merchants of Florence or the aldermen of Edward III's London. But there was also, as ever, political division. The Genoese were not popular with other Italians, perhaps because of their trading acumen and energy: Boccaccio called them 'men naturally and voraciously driven by attachment to money', and Dante in his *Inferno* put the Genovesi at the lowest point of hell.

Factional struggles within the Italian city states had diminished compared to the thirteenth century, but there was still conflict within ruling families that was often no less bloody, added to which conflicts between the states had if anything intensified. Genoa had a commercial power to rival Venice, with ships trading as far as Africa or the Crimea, yet complex rivalries were encouraging instability that within a generation would lead to the loss of Genoese independence and influence.

Genoa never did get its own English port, so in that sense Chaucer's trip – or at least that part of it – did not bear fruit. Relations between the Genoese and the locals in Southampton remained on the whole harmonious, but conflicts did break out, notably in 1379, when a Genoese ambassador, Janus Imperiale, travelled to London not only because a Genoese ship had been seized and looted at sea but also – and mainly – to pursue the lost cause of Southampton as an exclusive Genoese port, with wool exports avoiding the staple at Calais. Imperiale was murdered with a sword blow to his head by two assailants from the London Mercers' Guild while he was outside his lodgings in St Nicholas Acon Lane (now Nicholas Lane) near Lombard Street in the City.

As for di Mari, there is an intriguing reference in January 1376 to a 'Brother John de Mari' as a monk at Lenton Priory in Nottingham, recording that Brother John has the 'king's letters of exchange addressed to Peter Mark, merchant of Lumbardy dwelling in the city of London, for 10 marks payable to him in foreign parts'. Peter Mark was a representative of the Florentine Alberti family of bankers and traders in London. Three years earlier, in October 1373, 'John de Mare' had escaped from the Fleet prison in London. Edward III pardoned the prison governor, Walter Whithors (Whitehorse), who presumably paid to be exonerated, just as di Mari had no doubt paid Whithors (who was also custodian of the Palace of Westminster and Windsor Chapel) to let him out. Di Mari seems to have been confined in the Fleet on the king's own orders, 'to be kept in that prison until Walter shall have other orders from him'. Perhaps di Mari had cheated the Crown in matters of trade (or jewellery), or his wheeler-dealing had finally caught up with him; perhaps after escaping from the Fleet prison his penance was to take holy orders at Lenton Priory, while continuing to be useful to the government for his trading and banking connections. Lenton Priory had fine guest quarters and was much favoured by royal visitors, including Edward III.

Genoa also evidently continued to play a role in Chaucer's life: in August 1373, shortly after the trip to Italy, he was asked by Edward III to intervene when a Genoese ship, *La Seinte Marie et Seint George*, was detained at Dartmouth and the Genoese owner, a business associate of di Mari, demanded its return. Possibly Chaucer went down to Dartmouth himself to sort out this Genoese incident – and never forgot it, since Dartmouth is the home base of the Shipman in the *Canterbury Tales*.

6

Loans and Poems in Florence

Quite why Chaucer set off to Italy – a difficult journey in the Middle Ages at the best of times – in the icy depths of winter is not clear: possibly the question of relations with Genoa had become urgent following the defeat at La Rochelle and Edward III's decision to use Genoese expertise to bolster his navy. Equally likely is that Edward badly needed funding from Italian banks both in Genoa and in Florence, where he had defaulted on loans from the powerful Bardi banking family, and needed someone to mend fences.

As a consequence, the 1372–3 trip involved not only Genoa but also Florence – and it was there that Chaucer again came into contact with Italian literature. As John Tatlock noted over one hundred years ago, Chaucer had plenty of time to see both Petrarch and Boccaccio as well as deal with Genoese trade. It had previously been thought that Chaucer's journeys to Italy took two months there and two months back. But this was 'far too large an allowance', Tatlock wrote, since the historical records show that clerics took only a month to get from Dover to Aosta on their way to Rome. Altogether, Chaucer had over four months in Italy. Tatlock wrote:

These four or five months mean familiarity with the language, and that familiarity with the country (at various seasons, late winter, early spring, midsummer) which many travellers find stimulates an interest in its literature; they mean perhaps seeing his own countrymen with new eyes when he got home; they mean opportunities for procuring books.

This does not mean, Tatlock continued, that 'as he rode homeward his saddle-bags were bulging with the hundred best Italian books' or that he did not obtain Italian books from Italian merchants at the Custom House.

Picking up on Tatlock's point nearly forty years later, George Parks agreed that Chaucer's journeys must have taken no more than five weeks each way, leaving considerably more time for the sojourn in Italy than had been supposed. More recently, Wendy Childs has pointed out that the journey by sea with Genoese or Venetian trading fleets would have taken no more than eight weeks in good weather, but 'the risks of adverse winds, wreck and piracy, and the well-attested cramped and smelly conditions of medieval ships made the quicker and more reliable land routes more attractive to all who could choose'. Childs adds:

The routes through France and Germany and over the Alps were well trodden by generations of travellers, and there was no difficulty about finding the way ... The Alps naturally posed difficulties in winter, but local guides could keep travellers moving ... Chaucer himself had to

cross the Alps in winter when he left England for Italy on
1 December 1372.

In travelling from London to Genoa and Florence, Chaucer
would almost certainly have thought of following the route
taken by Prince Lionel to Milan in 1368 by way of Paris, Savoy,
and Mont Cenis. But England's war with France had revived
in 1369, so the route through France was almost certainly
closed to Chaucer's party.

There were no reliable maps in Chaucer's time: he refers
once to a *mappa mundi* of the kind still to be seen at Her-
eford Cathedral, but that was a divine rather than practical
guide, with Jerusalem at its centre. There were, on the other
hand, well-trodden routes known to traders and bishops: as
Margaret Wade Labarge notes in *Medieval Travellers*, modern
tourists wrongly imagine that 'no one in the remote Middle
Ages ever went far from home or indulged themselves in
foreign travel', when in fact this was untrue: in 1390–1, John
of Gaunt's son Henry of Derby, the future Henry IV, went to
Lithuania, Konigsberg (Kaliningrad), and Danzig (Gdansk)
with the crusading Teutonic Knights, then to the Holy Land
via Venice, stopping at Prague to see King Wenceslas, and
returned to England via Turin, crossing the Alps at the Mont
Cenis pass to Chambery, Macon, Troyes, and Paris.

In December 1372, Chaucer presumably went via the Low
Countries and Germany – that is to say, the merchant route
from Calais to Bruges, Ghent, Maastricht, and Aachen, to the
Rhine at Cologne or Bonn, then to Basel and south to Lake
Geneva at Lausanne. He then had three choices – Geneva

and Chambery to Mont Cenis; the Great St Bernard Pass to Aosta and then Turin or Chivasso, 'one of the oldest and most frequented routes to and from Italy'; or the Simplon Pass across the Alps to Lake Maggiore and Milan, though this was less likely because of conflict between Savoy and Milan. The Alpine passes were kept open in winter despite ice and snow, freezing cold, and howling winds, with travellers praying to Saint Julian, the patron saint of hospitality, to help them find refuge and avoid dying from exposure to the elements, as Chaucer himself notes in the *House of Fame*. The distance was about 1,600 km, which took merchants up to a month, though some took longer. So Chaucer probably left on 1 December 1372 and arrived sometime between 1 and 10 January 1373. For the return journey in April and May, he probably took the same route back, given that Milan was still under attack from Savoy and papal armies. He left Genoa between 13 and 23 April to arrive back in London on 23 May. France would still have been closed to him, since John of Gaunt was preparing to march from Calais to Bordeaux.

The most likely time for a visit to Arqua to see Petrarch was therefore between 17 and 27 April 1373. Parks wrote:

> We cannot say whether he did see Petrarch. We can say whether he could have seen him. The answer is that he could. Indeed, a route home by or close to Arqua turns out to be almost the only alternative route open to him if he did not go home as he came out.

Equally possible is that Chaucer saw Petrarch at Cervara,

between Santa Margherita and Portofino, where Petrarch's close friend Guido Sette, the archbishop of Genoa, had built a Benedictine monastery, San Girolamo della Cervara. By the time of Chaucer's visit, Sette was dead, but Petrarch would have regarded Cervara – with its breathtaking gardens and coastal views – as his second home. The abbey, as it became, is now privately owned but open to groups by arrangement, and is a favoured setting for weddings.

The journey from Genoa to Florence would have taken Chaucer through Pisa: in 'The Monk's Tale', he tells the story of Count Ugolino of Pisa, taken from Dante's *Inferno*, in which Ugolino and his children are condemned to die in a tower 'a little way out of Pisa' (this is presumably not the twelfth-century Leaning Tower, which is in the centre of the city). Chaucer would probably also have passed through Lucca, where he may well have encountered Giovanni Sercambi, one of whose stories bears a remarkable resemblance to Chaucer's 'Shipman's Tale' in the *Canterbury Tales*.

But the journey in the fourteenth century was not exactly the Tuscan idyll of today: Chaucer would have been very aware that Northern Italy was torn by local conflicts in this period. One of the leading protagonists, after all, was the English mercenary John Hawkwood, said to be one of the models for 'The Knight's Tale', whom Chaucer may have met at the 1368 Milan wedding, and whom he certainly met on his next Italian trip. In 1368, Chaucer, writes Frances Stonor Saunders, was 'a humble squire' to whom Hawkwood and others would not have paid much attention. But five years later he was 'an established and valued presence in the English court, honoured with gifts of winter and summer robes, as well as robes of mourning, appropriate to his degree'.

The impact of Italy on Chaucer, when he finally arrived, would have been life-changing: Milan was one thing, with its castles and monuments, but the Italian countryside was quite another. Chaucer would have been struck in Italy – and above all in Florence – by the landscape, the light of the Tuscan sun, the architecture, and the art. It was after this journey that Chaucer increasingly used Italian as well as French literature as his source and inspiration.

He also discovered Dante and his *Divine Comedy*. Chaucer would already no doubt have heard of Dante from the Italian merchants in London, but it was in 1373 that Boccaccio, Dante's most devoted disciple, persuaded the Florentine authorities to honour the great poet they had voted into exile some seventy years before with a series of commemorative lectures, given by Boccaccio himself at the Florentine church of Santo Stefano di Badia. The lectures were given in October, after Chaucer had returned to England, but they would have been the talk of the town during his visit.

Chaucer's visit to Florence emerges not from the recorded commission from the king but rather from the travel expenses he submitted afterwards. The purpose of the journey may have had to do with the supply of ships to England by Florentine merchants, as well as with Edward III's request for a loan from the Bardi bank in Florence. The Bardi Company headquarters was in Via de' Bardi between the Ponte Vecchio and the Ponte alle Grazie, on the 'other side' of the River Arno ('Oltrarno'). The fortunes of the Bardi family began in the thirteenth century, when it inherited a castle and land at Vernio, some 32 km from Florence. By the early fourteenth century, the Compagnia dei Bardi was the main bank in Europe, providing wool merchants and other traders with bills of exchange (an early form of cheques) and, of course, loans, together with the equally powerful Peruzzi family of Florentine bankers. Chaucer would have been well aware that, in the 1340s, Edward III was said to have ruined the Bardis by failing to pay them debts estimated at between 1 million and 1.5 million gold florins.

Some accounts suggest that this was exaggerated, however. Edward III did repay at least some of the debt – enough to make a further loan possible thirty years later, in the 1370s, though full settlements to the Bardi Company by the royal court for unpaid debts did not take place until 1392. Edwin Hunt argues that Edward III was clearly 'a man with little talent for attracting, at reasonable cost, the vast sums of money needed to carry out his ambitious political ventures' but has questioned the scale of Edward's debts. Chaucer's 'secret business' for the king in Florence almost certainly involved trying to negotiate new war loans from the Bardis, who were, after all, powerful international bankers with offices not only in Florence but also in Jerusalem, Constantinople, Tunis, Cyprus, and Rhodes, as well as Spain and France.

Florence, in other words, was an Italian financial and industrial powerhouse with which England needed to create – and keep – alliances. Florence had an economy based on banking and luxury textiles such as wool and silk, and it was ruled by an oligarchy of nobles and merchant families including the Medici, who in the next century formed a powerful dynasty that was to rule a flourishing Florence. As Ross King has noted:

> Bales of English wool – the finest in the world – were brought from monasteries in the Cotswolds to be washed in the river Arno, combed, spun into yarn, woven on wooden looms, then dyed beautiful colours: vermilion, made from cinnabar gathered on the shores of the Red Sea, or a brilliant yellow procured from the crocuses growing in meadows near the hilltop town of San Gimignano. The result was the most expensive and most sought-after cloth in Europe.

Since the end of the thirteenth century, Florence had been run by the *popolo* – a term referring not to the general public but to the seven major guilds (the *Arti Maggiori*, which elected the magistrates who ran the legal system): bankers and money changers; judges, lawyers and notaries; traders in cloth; wool merchants; doctors and apothecaries; and the silk and fur merchants. There were also fourteen *Arti Minori*, including blacksmiths, carpenters, stonemasons, butchers, shoemakers, wine merchants, saddlers, locksmiths, armourers, bakers, and innkeepers.

The gold florin of Florence and the gold ducat of Venice were the principal units of international currency. Instead of a pope or emperor, the florin carried the image of a lily on one side and of John the Baptist (the patron saint of Florence) on the other. Chianti began to emerge as a classic Tuscan red wine in the fourteenth century, with villages between Florence and Siena forming a league, the *Lega del Chianti*, with a black cock or rooster against a golden background as their emblem.

Chaucer would have been impressed by Florence's prosperity, its fortified walls and towers, and its ambitious building programme: with a population (like Genoa) of some 100,000, Florence held twice as many people as London. Its cathedral, or duomo, of Santa Maria del Fiore was mostly constructed in the fourteenth century, with houses and markets cleared to make room for it. Although its magnificent dome, designed by Filippo Brunelleschi, did not go up until 1436, the duomo Chaucer saw was still awe-inspiring, with the campanile, or bell tower, designed by Giotto soaring into the Florentine sky.

The ancient Baptistery of St John beside it, founded in the fourth century as a basilica by St Ambrose on the ruins of a Roman temple, had been given its green-and-white marble facade in the twelfth century, and in 1328 Andrea Pisano designed its splendid bronze south doors, with their illustrations of stories from the Bible, completed ten years later and supplemented by the intricate carvings of Lorenzo Ghiberti on the north and east doors.

Much of the medieval Florence that Chaucer experienced still survives – including the Bargello, originally the palazzo for magistrates and police and now a museum; impressive merchants' houses; numerous churches such as Santa Maria Novella, San Lorenzo, Santa Croce, and the Convent of San Marco; and the Via del Corso, the main shopping street, at that time often the scene of horse races competing for the *palio*, a standard of red brocade bearing the arms of the city.

89

Impressive, too, was the Ponte Vecchio, the former Roman bridge across the Arno that was rebuilt in 1345 after floods, which was (and still is) lined with shops, originally butchers and tanners and nowadays jewellers and souvenir-sellers. The Ponte Vecchio is still one of the great sights of Florence, as is the Palazzo Vecchio, the fortress-like city hall with a crenellated tower on the Piazza della Signoria, a spacious paved piazza where in medieval times heavy carts were banned, along with begging, sex work, and street gambling. The Palazzo Vecchio, designed by Arnolfo di Cambio, was built to represent the power of the commune and the guilds that controlled it, its striking bell tower reaching into the sky. Florence had eighty banks processing the revenues from the wool and cloth trades. There was civil unrest in Florence when the downtrodden *ciompi* (wool carders) marched on the Palazzo Vecchio to protest against their poor pay and miserable work conditions, but it was short-lived, and the merchant classes soon reimposed control.

The word '*vecchio*' means old, but the Florentine bridges and palaces would have been breathtakingly new to Chaucer. And then there was the heritage of Giotto: the great painter had died in 1337 but, as the art historian Giorgio Vasari later wrote, he had revolutionised painting by 'drawing accurately from life'. Chaucer would have admired not just Giotto's campanile but also his frescoes at the Bardi Chapel in the Franciscan Basilica of Santa Croce.

One of the most pressing factors behind Chaucer's visit to Florence, after all, was the link between Edward III and Florentine merchants and bankers such as the aristocratic Bardi family, which was influential in both Florence and London – so influential, in fact, that Walter de Bardi became master of the mint for both Edward III and Richard II. Boccaccio's father worked for the Bardi Company in Florence and later in Naples, as for a while did Boccaccio himself, and there are a number of admiring references to Giotto and painting in the *Decameron*.

It is more than likely that Chaucer attended Mass in the Bardi Chapel, with its frescoes by Giotto depicting St Francis, which at the time were gloriously new and which can still be admired today (the frescoes were whitewashed over in the eighteenth century but restored in the nineteenth and twentieth centuries). As Marion Turner puts it:

> Given Chaucer's interest in culture, the compact nature of Florence, the centrality of worship to everyday life, and the close relationship between the Bardi family and Santa Croce, the overwhelming likelihood is that Chaucer saw the art of Giotto and consciously experienced the artistic revolution that had taken place.

He would also have admired the fourteenth-century Bardi Chapel at the church of Santa Maria Novella, where Boccaccio's pilgrims gather before setting off for a villa outside the city to escape the plague.

This points to an aspect of Chaucer's visit to Florence that would have a rather more lasting impact than simply renegotiating loans: Chaucer, after all, was a literary pioneer, the first of numerous English writers over the centuries to draw inspiration from Florence. As Charles Hobday observes in *A Golden Ring*, his study of English writers in Florence, 'Ever since Chaucer visited Florence on a diplomatic mission and discovered the poetry of Dante, Petrarch, and Boccaccio, English poets have been conducting a love affair with the city.'

Above all, the trip would have given Chaucer a chance to encounter at least one of his three Italian sources – a man who was born near Florence; who was the son of a Florentine merchant who worked for the Bardi family; who carried out diplomatic missions for Florence, including one to Pope Urban V; who entertained Petrarch on behalf of the city at his Florence home, and who at the time of Chaucer's visit was revising his *Decameron*: Giovanni Boccaccio.

7

Giovanni Boccaccio

'A notorious puzzle in Geoffrey Chaucer's poetry is his refusal to name Giovanni Boccaccio,' Karen Gross has observed. It is indeed a mystery, for there can be no doubt that Boccaccio was one of Chaucer's major influences, and there can be no less doubt – in my view – that their paths crossed in Italy.

Boccaccio had been about fifty-five at the time of the Milan wedding in 1368, and he was nearly sixty at the time of Chaucer's visit to Florence in 1373. Boccaccio was therefore an established figure from whom the thirty-one-year-old Chaucer could learn a great deal. Like Chaucer, he was not only a writer but was also sent on sensitive missions – in Boccaccio's case, on behalf of Florence. His father, Boccaccino di Chellino, was a Florentine merchant who worked for the Bardi Company and was a member of the powerful Florence guild of bankers and money-changers; his mother is unknown, and may have been Boccaccino's first wife – either that or Boccaccio was the result of an extramarital affair, which at the time was neither uncommon nor seen as a disadvantage.

Boccaccio spent his last years in the small Tuscan town of Certaldo, 35 km from Florence, surrounded by rolling hills, cypress trees, and olive groves, and close to the Via Francigena, the pilgrim route from Canterbury to Rome. Certaldo – which is nowadays twinned, appropriately enough, with Canterbury – is divided into lower and upper towns, with a statue of Boccaccio in the main piazza in the lower town. But his home, the Casa Boccaccio, is in the medieval upper town, Certaldo Alto, which retains its fortified walls and is reached by a funicular railway. Boccaccio set one of his *Decameron* stories in the town, noting in the opening to the story that 'Certaldo, as you may possibly have heard, is a little town in the Val d'Elsa, in the hinterland of Florence', and adding that, although it was small in size, Certaldo was 'once the home of wealthy and noble people' (*Decameron* 6:10).

Boccaccio refers in the story to the local delicacy, which he must have enjoyed many times: the tasty red and purple onions of Certaldo, used for jam; ribollita (broth); pâté on toast; and spaghetti *alla cipolla*, cooked with the local onions that, Boccaccio boasts, are '*famose per tutta Toscana*' ('famous throughout Tuscany'). His tale features a monk called Frate Cipolla ('brother onion'), who deals in fake relics – notably the feathers of the angel Gabriel – but who, being small, red-haired, merry, and quick-witted, is welcomed in Certaldo, in the first instance 'probably on account of his name'. The onion even features on the town's medieval coat of arms, a red-and-white split shield featuring an onion and bearing the motto '*Per natura sono forte e dolce ancora, e piaccio a chi sta e a chi lavora*' ('by nature I am still strong and sweet, and I please those who stay and work'). In July there is still a five-day festival of jugglers, musicians, and dancers called the Mercantia, and every October local people dress up in medieval costume for the Certaldo food festival, the Boccaccesca, which features not only red onions but also white truffles, olive oil, and Chianti.

Boccaccio's house, in what is now Via Boccaccio, was largely destroyed in the Second World War by Allied bombing but has been faithfully reconstructed in local red brick. Its features include a library and an exhibition of Boccaccio's life and work, with views from the house's tower across the Tuscan landscape of the Val d'Elsa towards San Gimignano. Other nearby sights include the medieval Palazzo Pretorio, its facade decorated with ceramic coats of arms, which in Boccaccio's time was a prison and court of justice, and a former Augustinian convent which is now the Museo di Arte Sacra ('museum of sacred art').

Boccaccio is buried in the nearby church of Santi Jacopo e Filippo. Whether Boccaccio's birth on 16 June or July 1313 took place there as well as his death sixty-two years later is unclear: Edward Hutton, who lived at the Villa di Boccaccio at Settignano, near Florence, was a founder of the British Institute of Florence and published his biography of Boccaccio in 1910. He argued that Boccaccio was conceived while his father was in Paris on business and that he was probably born there rather than in Certaldo, an assertion shared by a number of Italian scholars.

In the 1320s, Boccaccio's father married Margherita dei Mardoli, who came from a prosperous noble family and thus became Boccaccio's well-to-do stepmother. In 1326, Boccaccio's father was appointed head of the Bardi bank in Naples and moved there with his family. Boccaccio duly became an apprentice at the bank, but swiftly decided that banking was not for him and convinced his father to let him study law at the Studium (now the University of Naples) instead, where he became a student of canon law for six years.

His father introduced him to the Neapolitan nobility and the court of the king of Naples, Robert the Wise of the Anjou dynasty. In Naples, he fell in love with Robert's beautiful (and illegitimate) daughter, Maria d'Aquino, while attending Mass. Unfortunately, Maria was already married, but she none the less became the figure Fiammetta ('little flame') depicted in the *Teseida* and the *Filostrato*, and as one of the narrators in the *Decameron* – in other words, Boccaccio's counterpart to Petrarch's Laura. His *Elegia di Madonna Fiammetta* is considered the first psychological novel and, much later, his passion for her inspired the Pre-Raphaelite artist Dante Gabriel Rossetti to paint *A Vision of Fiammetta*, portraying her as a striking redhead, as her nickname would suggest.

Boccaccio was no more suited to law than banking, but his studies at least allowed him to pursue his interest in scientific and literary studies. By his own account, his early mentors included Paolo da Perugia, the author of a collection of myths; Barbato da Sulmona, King Robert's chancellor, to whom Petrarch dedicated a volume of Latin verses; Giovanni Barrili, a magistrate and diplomat; and the theologian Dionigi di Borgo San Sepolcro.

Above all, it was in Naples that Boccaccio found his true calling: poetry. It was during his Neapolitan years that he wrote the *Filostrato* and the *Teseida,* which, respectively, form the basis for Chaucer's *Troilus and Criseyde* and 'The Knight's

Tale'; the *Filocolo*, a prose rewriting of a French romance; and the poem *La caccia di Diana*. Once again, politics intervened, however, with growing tensions over the Naples Anjou dynasty's role in the affairs of Florence, and Boccaccio returned to his native city early in 1341. His father had already returned three years earlier, though in much reduced circumstances, having gone bankrupt. Boccaccio thus narrowly missed an epidemic or 'pestilence' that had struck Florence in 1340 and killed thousands of residents (though appearing not long before the Black Death, this disease apparently was not related to it). But, much to his chagrin, he also missed the visit of Petrarch to that city in 1341 to be crowned (again) Poet Laureate. Back in Florence, Boccaccio produced *Comedia delle ninfe fiorentine* (also known as *Ameto*), composed of both prose and poetry, in 1341; completed an allegorical poem entitled *Amorosa visione* (thought to have been an inspiration for Chaucer's *House of Fame*) in 1342; and, the following year, published his *Elegy of Fiammetta*.

The politics of Florence remained an issue, however: crippled by mounting debts and the conflict between Black and White Guelphs, the Florentines had turned for support to Robert of Naples and his son Charles, Duke of Calabria, and then to Walter of Brienne, the Duke of Athens. However, Walter ruled autocratically, imposed punishing taxes, and altogether alienated the very merchant guilds that had put him in power in the first place, and was forced to leave Florence by a furious population, barely escaping with his life.

A further blow to Florence came with the arrival in 1348 of the Black Death, which killed half the city's population. It is hardly surprising, therefore, that Boccaccio left for Ravenna and Forli, beginning the *Decameron* in 1349 and completing its one hundred tales over the next three years, though he was to revise the collection much later, in the early 1370s – the time of Chaucer's visit to Florence.

We know he was back in Florence by 1350, because in October of that year – having missed Petrarch's visit to Naples – he was delegated to greet the great Poet Laureate as he entered Florence and have him as his guest at his home. Nothing could have given Boccaccio greater pleasure: Willard Farnham suggests that their friendship has been 'over-sentimentalised', but Petrarch was Boccaccio's teacher and *magister* ('master') and encouraged him to study classical Greek and Latin literature. They met again in Padua the following year, when Boccaccio was sent on an official mission to invite Petrarch to take a chair at the University of Florence. He was unsuccessful, but once again their discussions bore fruit, this time in the form of Boccaccio's *Genealogia deorum gentilium*, a study of ancient literature and philosophy that was to remain a definitive work on classical mythology for hundreds of years.

At the heart of the work was Boccaccio's firm belief – clearly adopted from Petrarch – that humanist values and pagan traditions were not at odds with Christian values and beliefs but complemented them. That Boccaccio held deep religious beliefs there can be no doubt: he seems to have undergone some kind of spiritual crisis in 1359, following a meeting that year with Pope Innocent VI and a later mission to Pope Urban V in Avignon, and is even believed to have taken holy orders, or at least some form of Catholic office.

In 1359, Boccaccio again met Petrarch, this time in Milan,

when Boccaccio was named Florentine ambassador to the court of the Viscontis – hence his (and Petrarch's) presence at the 1368 wedding of Lionel of Antwerp and Violante Visconti, which, as we have seen, Chaucer may well have helped to organise. In 1360, Boccaccio began work on *De mulieribus claris*, the biographies of 106 famous women both real and mythological, from Eve to Juno, Sappho, Cleopatra, and Zenobia – though he did not complete them until 1374, the year before his death.

In 1361, Boccaccio went back to Certaldo: there had been a failed coup in Florence, and although Boccaccio (as far as we know) was not directly involved in it, a number of his close friends were, and they were exiled or executed in the purge that followed. He was further troubled when a monk famed for his prophecies and miracles, Pietro de Petroni from Maggiano, near Lucca, claimed when he was dying that he had had a vision of the 'souls of the damned', one of whom was Boccaccio. A fellow monk, Gioacchini Ciani, took the message to Boccaccio in 1362 and warned him to repent, but Petrarch persuaded him that deathbed visions were hallucinations.

For the next four years, Boccaccio (understandably) carried out no further diplomatic missions for Florence, but he did go to Naples, Padua, and Venice in 1365, meeting Petrarch at his residence in Venice. In 1367, when the papacy finally returned to Rome from Avignon, Boccaccio was sent by Florence to congratulate Pope Urban (although Urban only stayed for three years before returning to Avignon; it was Gregory XI who fully restored the papacy in Rome).

He met Petrarch again in Padua in 1368, and when Petrarch died in July 1374 Boccaccio wrote a commemorative poem.

He did not have long to live himself, however: he was increasingly in poor health and increasingly obese. He had apparently considered burning his archive of letters, books, and manuscripts, but was persuaded not to do so by Petrarch, who even offered to buy them from him. In the event, Boccaccio left his library and archive in his will to the Convent (now Basilica) of Santo Spirito, across the Arno in Florence, which he had often attended, holding meetings there with other early humanists. His final years were troubled not only by his weight but also by fevers and dropsy, a swelling of the tissues that we would now call oedema, often a sign of heart failure. He died at the age of sixty-two on 21 December 1375 in Certaldo, where he is buried.

Chaucer was clearly guided by Boccaccio and, as Donald Howard argues in his life of Chaucer, it would take a series of inconceivable coincidences to allow us to conclude that Chaucer did *not* know Boccaccio. For Howard, the following coincidences would have to have taken place: 'by serendipity', Boccaccio's works would have somehow happened to have fallen into Chaucer's hands, and he would have just happened to have made adaptations of them; a few other of Boccaccio's works, also by complete chance, would have to have just fallen into Chaucer's hands, and he then to have quoted from them; and Chaucer would have, again quite by chance, to have imitated several of Boccaccio's works, such as the *Decameron*; Chaucer was in Florence when Boccaccio was also there, so something would have to have prevented the two great poets from meeting each other; moreover, Chaucer knew the famous Visconti family, as did Boccaccio, so a meeting between the two of them would have to have been somehow precluded despite this high-profile mutual connection. Moreover, as David Wallace has observed, Chaucer 'made more use of Boccaccio than of any other writer', with both men drawing on the 'great authors of antiquity' while at the same time appealing to 'a broad range of readers' by adopting a popular and easy-going style.

There is no evidence that copies of the *Decameron* reached England during Chaucer's lifetime: the earliest known copy was obtained in 1414 – in French, not Italian – by Humphrey, Duke of Gloucester, an ardent book collector who gave his collection to the University of Oxford, forming the basis of what became the Bodleian Library. But then, as Donald McGrady has noted, it is not only Boccaccio's manuscripts that are missing, since no copies of the *Canterbury Tales*, or indeed any other works by Chaucer, survive from his own day. 'To dispose of the argument that a lack of fourteenth-century manuscripts indicates that the *Decameron* was not known in England, we need only recall that no manuscripts of any of Chaucer's own works survive from that time either,' McGrady comments. 'Why should we expect other manuscripts, older than Chaucer's to begin with, to last longer than his?' Chaucer, moreover, knew Italian, and if he did have a copy he would have obtained it in Italian either from his merchant contacts in London – many of whom were Florentines – or on his travels in Italy. The *Decameron* was widely known and imitated in Chaucer's lifetime, not least in Italy itself by Giovanni Sercambi, Giovanni Fiorentino, Franco Sacchetti, and Simone de' Prodenzani.

One suggestion is that Chaucer's reference in *Troilus* to '*myn auctor Lollius*' is an oblique reference to Boccaccio, the name Lollius being a pun on 'lolling', or bad-mouthing (in Italian, '*boca-accio*'ing), though for Karen Gross this is 'tortuous and far-fetched'. But there are other clues that show Chaucer was well acquainted with the works of Boccaccio, such as Arcite in 'The Knight's Tale' calling himself 'Philostrate' (*Filostrato*).

A possible explanation for Chaucer's failure to acknowledge Boccaccio is that he considered him – unlike Petrarch – to be a vernacular author, not a Latin one, and therefore felt that he did not carry the authorial heft to be singled out as an *auctore* ('author'). Chaucer's 'strange silence' about Boccaccio has even led some critics to propose that he did not in fact know who the author of the *Teseida*, the *Filostrato*, the *Filocolo*, and the *Decameron* actually was. Willard Farnham suggests that Boccaccio himself came to regret the 'lascivious' *Decameron* – and writing it in 'vulgar' Italian rather than Latin – and so downplayed it, which 'may help to explain why the *Decameron* was oddly slow in getting itself known by Europe'.

But for Donald McGrady 'the truth of the matter is quite the opposite', since the *Decameron* was widely imitated in Italy and was certainly 'well known in other European countries'. The picture of Boccaccio as 'anguished by his youthful rashness in composing such a wicked collection' is, for him, an 'egregious flight of fancy'. It also strikes Karen Gross as 'special pleading' to suggest Chaucer did not know about Boccaccio, since Chaucer was 'far too well read to be ignorant of the name of the author of so many works he used'. She writes, 'Chaucer's mysterious game of silence about the writer who had the largest influence upon him is symptomatic of his relationship with the Italian tradition as a whole: namely its quietude.' Or, as Marion Turner concludes, 'Most critics would now accept that Chaucer knew the *Decameron* in some form.'

A more plausible scenario is that Chaucer did indeed read Boccaccio, and probably met him, but simply chose not to make a point of it. In other words, he could never quite bring himself to admit his debt. 'Quietude', after all, is serenity, tranquillity, peace: in other words, Chaucer absorbed Italian literature in Milan, Florence, and Padua, but saw no reason to make a song and dance about it. It was simply part of his imaginative framework. Chaucer shared with Boccaccio and other Italian writers a fascination with dream landscapes, the use of space, and what the Greeks called '*ekphrasis*', the way in which writers describe or reflect works of art such as paintings or sculptures.

Moreover, the *Decameron* was well known in Europe during Chaucer's lifetime, and, as we have seen, Chaucer had almost certainly learned Italian before going to Italy – in fact, it was probably this that made him an ideal choice as an envoy to Italy. It was the *Decameron*, David Wallace suggests in *A Companion to Chaucer*, that 'clearly inspired Chaucer's swerve away from the court-centred poetics that had dominated the first half of his career': he was 'a brilliantly gifted Italianist who understood complex clauses of Boccaccio's poetry that still cause modern translators to stumble'. As for *Troilus and Criseyde*, Chaucer's version of Boccaccio's *Filostrato*, Wallace writes, close examination of the texts clearly shows that

Chaucer 'directly engaged with Boccaccio's text in minute local detail'. Perhaps 'by instinct', Peter Ackroyd suggests, Chaucer simply 'knew that the Italian poet was too close a source and inspiration to be confessed to the world'. For Paul Strohm, Chaucer 'certainly knew and enjoyed access to' Boccaccio's works, including the *Teseida* and the *Filostrato*, and was 'either the only native English writer or literary enthusiast of the 1380s to know these works, or one of very few'. But his 'heavy reliance upon Boccaccio is uncredited and, it must be said, wilfully concealed', not least because Chaucer had 'a concealed but highly active sense of rivalry with his better established Italian competitor'. Chaucer's relationship with Boccaccio was therefore 'fraught with unmistakable symptoms of envy', Strohm concludes. For Donald McGrady, it may belabour the obvious 'to say that a fourteenth-century author perhaps did not feel it appropriate to recognise publicly his indebtedness to writings of popular entertainment, composed by a contemporary, and in the vernacular'. He writes, 'It also seems reasonable to assume that his residence of several months in that country would have been sufficient for him to discover one of the current best sellers.' But he had probably been lent or given them, in any case, by one of the many merchants, bankers, and diplomats in London who were Florentines and therefore compatriots of Boccaccio. In other words, Chaucer knew what the creative geniuses of Italy such as Petrarch and Boccaccio were producing *before he even went there*. And, as a budding author, he would certainly have been keen to meet them.

8

The Knight's Tale

To see quite how much Chaucer took from Boccaccio – while developing the stories with his own particular English genius – it is worth taking a closer look at the two writers' work. Chaucer did not, of course, simply imitate the Italian output: after all, he was writing for an English audience. There were aspects of the writings of Dante, Petrarch, and Boccaccio that he did not make use of, including their fascination with classical culture; the typical presence of a beatific lady with a supernatural influence on the poet; commentary on one's own work as if it had some kind of scriptural authority; and the presentation of poetry as divinely inspired. Chaucer did refer to classical antiquity: he knew the *Filostrato* was set in Troy and the *Teseida* (the story of Theseus) in Thebes in ancient Greece, and his 'Monk's Tale' is based on Boccaccio's *De casibus virorum illustrium,* in which pagan generals and rulers come to a bad end. He also quotes Seneca, Cicero, and Livy. But he did not pick up the other elements of Italian literature, such as the ennobling love of a sublime lady (apart, perhaps, from Blanche in the *Book of the Duchess*): Dante had his Beatrice, Petrarch his Laura, and Boccaccio his Fiammetta, whereas Chaucer had Alison, the Wife of Bath. Jill Mann has pointed out that many of Chaucer's stories apart from 'The Knight's Tale' have a woman as their central character, and one of the themes of the *Canterbury Tales* is what a good marriage consists of. But there is no Beatrice, and no Laura or Fiammetta, for that matter. The Wife of Bath is 'old, unattractive, sexually available, and delightfully vulgar'.

For Karen Gross, it is a puzzling paradox to suggest that 'the writer who best knew what the Italians were doing systematically rejected their innovations, and in doing so changed the course of English letters'. 'It is a commonplace of Chaucer scholarship that Chaucer's oeuvre can be divided roughly between those works that he wrote before his exposure to Italian literature and those he wrote afterward,' Gross writes. But his familiarity with Italian works is 'surprisingly broad: he knows the entire *Commedia*, the story of Griselda, the *De casibus virorum illustrium* of Boccaccio.' These continental bestsellers were 'not necessarily so well known in England'. Chaucer even knew Dante's little-known work *Convivio,* which the Wife of Bath quotes extensively when discussing *gentillesse,* suggesting that Chaucer's acquaintance with Italian letters was not a casual one'. How did Chaucer recognise that Boccaccio had misquoted Dante? Obviously because he knew the original. No other writer of the time 'looked to Italy for artistic inspiration' in the same way, Gross concludes.

Chaucer clearly knew all of Boccaccio's works: the opening to 'The Monk's Tale' mentions *De casibus*, a direct reference to Boccaccio: '*Here bigynneth the Monkes Tale, De casibus virorum illustrium*'; the same Tale includes the stories of

Adam; Sampson; Hercules; Nebuchadnezzar; Zenobia, Queen of Palmyra; Nero; Alexander; and Julius Caesar, all drawn from Boccaccio's *De casibus virorum illustrium*. Chaucer's *Troilus and Criseyde* – and ultimately Shakespeare's *Troilus and Cressida* too – derives from Boccaccio's *Filostrato*, in which the Trojan hero Troilus falls in love with Criseyde (or Cressida), daughter of the Trojan prophet Calchas, who has defected to the Greeks. Criseyde's cousin Pandarus (in Chaucer's version, he is Criseyde's uncle) offers to act as a go-between, and Troilus and Criseyde duly get together, but she then falls for a Greek hero, Diomedes, while pretending to be still in love with Troilus, who tries to kill Diomedes in battle but is himself killed by Achilles. Chaucer wrote his version shortly after returning from his trip to Italy in 1378, and must have had the *Filostrato* with him. There are differences: for one thing, as Marion Turner has pointed out, Chaucer focuses much more attention on Troy (often used at the time as a metaphor for London) as internally divided than does Boccaccio: 'The attractive surface of Troy, with its dinner parties, book groups and festivals is everywhere offset by political and personal betrayals, secret stratagems, intimations of rape, and aggressive and bloody imagery'. But, although there are significant differences in the two versions, Barry Windeatt has noted close similarities:

> For long stretches *Troilus* follows *Filostrato* so closely that Chaucer must have worked with a copy of the Italian in front of him as he created the draft of his poem ... Over and over again, the first line of Chaucer's

stanzas is very closely rendered from the parallel Italian
line, stanza by stanza.

For Peter Ackroyd, 'all the evidence suggests that he had the
volume open before him, since there are many line-by-line
translations which could not have been accomplished by
memory alone'.

The most telling example of Chaucer's debt to Boccaccio
is 'The Knights Tale', which is based on Boccaccio's *Il Teseida
delle Nozze d'Emilia* ('the Theseid concerning the nuptials
of Emily'). The *Teseida* has nearly 10,000 lines, while 'The
Knight's Tale' has only 2,250 lines – although it is still one of
the longer *Canterbury Tales*. For Ackroyd, the resemblances
'are so close and continuous that Chaucer could not have
relied upon a free memory of earlier reading; he must have
had the manuscripts to hand, and worked upon them line
by line or stanza by stanza'. Like 'The Knight's Tale', Boccaccio's *Teseida* tells the story of the ancient Greek hero Teseo
(Theseus) and the rivalry of two knights, Palemone and
Arcita, who are cousins, for the love of Emilia. In Boccaccio's
version, the Amazon warrior women of Scythia, on the Black
Sea, rebel against male rule and elect Ipolita (Hippolita) as
their queen. Teseo, Duke of Athens, launches an expedition,
defeats the warrior Amazon women, and makes Ipolita his
queen, but is attracted by the beauty of her sister Emilia.

Returning home to Athens with Ipolita, Teseo comes across
the widows of nobles and heroes defeated by the new ruler,
Creon of Thebes; he defeats Creon in battle and, finding two
cousins from the Theban royal family – Palemone and Arcita

– grievously injured on the battlefield, takes them back to Athens to be imprisoned for life. From the window of their shared prison cell, both men see Ipolita's younger sister, Emilia, and both are instantly smitten. Arcita is released from prison on condition that he will leave Athens and never return. Both men are now in agonies of unrequited love: Arcita because he is forbidden from returning to the city, and Palemone because he can see Emilia but is unable to be with her while he is imprisoned. As the years pass, Arcita's appearance changes as he gets older, so he decides to return to Athens under the name Penteo and secures a position in Teseo's court.

On learning of Arcita's illicit return, the imprisoned Palemone risks everything to escape and confronts his cousin in a grove. Their fight to the death is interrupted by Teseo, who by chance is leading a hunting party through the same grove. When he discovers the identities of the cousins and why they're fighting, he decrees that the two must fight it out in a tournament with a hundred knights each, and that the victor will win the hand of Emilia. He gives the two cousins a year to roam the world in search of knights to support them at the tournament.

A year later, the opposing champions arrive, and before the battle they pray to their chosen gods – as does Emilia, who, it turns out, has no wish to marry either of them and wants to remain single. Arcita wins without killing Palemone, marries Emilia, but dies from his wounds sustained in the fight and is given a hero's funeral. Teseo then decides that Emilia and Palemone should marry.

In his study of Chaucer's use of the *Teseida*, Robert Pratt notes that Boccaccio wrote his epic towards the end of his stay in Naples, in 1339–40, when his passion for Maria d'Aquino, his Fiammetta, 'seemed to have reached an almost hopeless conclusion'. He was studying a classical epic, the *Thebaid* (set in Thebes) by the first-century-AD Roman poet Publius Papinius Statius, who had lived and died in Naples, as part of his growing interest in the classics. Boccaccio evidently hoped his own classical epic would help to win d'Aquino's favour. He even consulted sailors and sailing charts before reconstructing Theseus's voyage from the Aegean to the Black Sea, but he was also guilty of absurdities such as making Theseus's theatre ten times larger than the Colosseum, and giving Emilia only one breast, though bizarrely she has two when she marries Arcita. But then, Pratt suggests, Boccaccio was seeking to combine a lofty epic style with 'episodes, characters and introspective analyses reflecting his own amatory experiences'. In a preface to the poem, Boccaccio tells his Fiammetta she will find both him and herself depicted in the poem, and hopes it will rekindle their lost flame of love.

Chaucer omits the first part of the *Teseida,* and he makes Theseus a more ruthless and less sympathetic character, but otherwise his narrative is not just similar, it is almost exactly the same. Theseus, the duke of 'fabled Athens', having returned from defeating the Amazons at Scythia with his Amazon queen, Hippolita, and her sister Emily (Emelye), defeats the local tyrant (Creon, king of Thebes), finds the cousins Palamon and Arcite unconscious on the battlefield, and has them imprisoned.

Their cell is in the tower of Theseus' castle, with a window that overlooks his palace garden. The imprisoned Palamon wakes early one morning in May and catches sight of Princess Emily, Theseus' sister-in-law, in the courtyard below, picking flowers for a garland. Palamon instantly falls in love with her; his moans are heard by Arcite, who wakes up, also sees Emily, and also falls in love with her. Palamon says he claimed her first, but Arcite replies that he has the right to love Emily as well, and their friendship becomes rivalry.

After some years, Arcite is released from prison on condition that he stays away from Athens, but he returns in disguise and becomes a servant in Emily's household in order to get close to her. Meanwhile, hearing that Arcite is back, Palamon drugs his jailer and makes his escape. Then, while hiding in a grove, he overhears Arcite singing about his love for Emily.

Their confrontation is interrupted by Theseus, who has them both arrested and plans to sentence them to death. Both his wife and Emily are against a death sentence, however, so instead Theseus finds a more elegant solution: they must compete in a tournament, with the victor winning the right to marry Emily. Palamon and Arcite each gather a hundred men for the tournament, and the night before the contest Palamon prays to Venus to win Emily's hand, while Arcite prays to Mars to help him win. Emily, for her part, prays to the goddess Diana that she may remain unmarried, or that, if she must marry, she will be the wife of the man who truly loves her.

The rules for the tournament lay down that if either man becomes seriously injured he must be taken out of the battle, and despite brave performances from both cousins, Palamon is wounded and unhorsed. Arcite is thus proclaimed the winner but, thanks to a divine intervention by Saturn, he is mortally wounded when his horse throws him off and then falls on him. As he lies dying, Arcite tells Emily that she should marry Palamon because he will make a good husband – and she does.

At first sight, Chaucer is simply copying Boccaccio, with sombre reflections inspired by the Greek classics on the nature of death as well as love. Theseus refers to the *primum movens* – the 'First Mover', who creates the 'Great Chain of Love' (in Chaucer, the '*faire cheyne of love*'), which holds fire, air, water, and earth together – and also to the inevitability of death for both men and nature. Theseus maintains that, since every man must die when his time comes, it is best to die with honour, as Arcite does. But Chaucer's version of the tale is much shorter than Boccaccio's – a quarter of the length – and much more concise, colourful, and gripping, with typically Chaucerian asides: when Palamon stays in prison while Arcite is freed, the Knight telling the tale remarks, 'Who could make rhymes in English fit to vie with martyrdom like that? Not I,' and later, 'It is well said that neither love nor power admits a rival, even for an hour, and Arcite and Palamon had found that out.' Chaucer's description of the tournament foreshadows his own later experiences of helping to stage such events as clerk of the King's Works, including the inclusion of craftsmen who build the great theatre for the knights' tournament – paid in both food and wages – and the painter who decorates a statue of the goddess Diana.

Chaucer's Knight, we are told, was just back from long service overseas, having fought for Christianity against the 'heathen infidels' in Alexandria, Russia, Lithuania, North Africa, Granada, and Anatolia. He was a 'true and noble knight' who had 'never said a boorish thing in his life' and was dressed for the pilgrimage to Canterbury not in his finery but in a stained fustian tunic 'with smudges where his armour had left a mark'. He tells the first story in the collection, after the pilgrims have drawn lots, and he appears to set the tone – but, in a Chaucerian touch, the Knight's narrative is followed not by another worthily classical epic but by the downright lewd 'Miller's Tale'. Like 'The Knight's Tale', 'The Miller's Tale' involves a conflict between two men – in the Miller's case, a carpenter and his student lodger – over a young woman, but it is completely the opposite in both tone and content: the Miller is clearly drunk after quaffing too much Southwark ale, he is 'straddling half on and half off his horse', and his story could hardly be further removed from classical mythology.

But then, 'The Miller's Tale' is also inspired by Boccaccio – this time not by the *Teseida* but by the *Decameron*.

9

Florence and Canterbury

The most obvious example of Chaucer's debt to Boccaccio is the way in which several of the *Canterbury Tales* are versions of the stories in the *Decameron* – or, to put it another way, they are what 'Canterbury' owes to 'Florence'. Boccaccio has his stories in the *Decameron* told by a group of rather genteel upper-class young men and women taking refuge from the plague at a villa just outside Florence, with servants and magnificent gardens. In Boccaccio's description, the place – said to be Settignano, later an Anglo-American colony favoured by writers and creatives such as Mark Twain, Gabriele d'Annunzio, Eleonora Duse, and Bernard Berenson – features lawns, gardens, and a palace with graceful paintings and 'cellars full of expensive wines'. By contrast, Chaucer's pilgrims – the Miller, the Shipman, the Friar, the Pardoner, the Merchant, the Cook, and so on – are ordinary people who set off from a tavern, and, unlike Boccaccio's characters, they are not especially religious, with there being no mention of them attending Mass or honouring the relics along the pilgrim route. The tales they tell, moreover, are often down to earth and risqué, not to say bawdy.

On the other hand, so too are many of the stories told by Boccaccio's supposedly refined refugees, so the two writers' imaginations are not that different, with both Boccaccio and Chaucer including disclaimers or apologies for including coarse stories. We have already seen how 'The Clerk's Tale' of Patient Griselda is based on the last story in the *Decameron*. Equally striking – and rather earthier in tone – is 'The Franklin's Tale', clearly derived from the fifth story on the tenth and last day of Boccaccio's *Decameron* (*Decameron* 10:5). Told by Emilia, one of the young ladies, it relates how Madonna Dianora, a married lady at Udine, in Friuli, has an ardent admirer called Baron Ansaldo Gradense. Exasperated by his advances, she finally says she will go to bed with him if in the cold month of January he can create a garden of grass, flowers, and trees 'in full leaf as if it were May' – and asks him, if he cannot do so, to please stop pestering her. The baron, realising he has been deliberately set an impossible task, none the less pays a necromancer to create a lovely garden by magic amid the snow and ice. Dianora, by now repenting of her promise, reveals all to her husband, who is at first furious but then tells her that, given the bargain she made, she can 'yield her body but not her soul' to her admirer. When she goes to Ansaldo, however, and tells him what her husband said, he is overcome with remorse and vows to honour her as his sister instead of making love to her: the magician, hearing this act of generosity, then forgoes his fee.

Chaucer sets his version of this story on the coast of Brittany rather than in Udine, and he includes numerous typically Chaucerian remarks, such as 'water will wear down the hardest stone'; 'if two lovers want to remain in love, they had better accede to each other's wishes'; and 'women, of their nature, crave for liberty; they will not be ordered around like servants' – adding, hastily, that 'men are the same, of course'. But the narrative is again very similar: the Franklin, a landowner below the rank of landed gentry who is also a local judge and fond of meat, fish, ale, and red wine, tells his fellow pilgrims the story of Dorigen, whose husband goes for two years from Brittany to Britain, 'the home of chivalry and adventure', leaving her to take lonely walks by the sea in her distress. To cheer Dorigen up, her friends take her to a dance, where she meets Aurelius, a young man – handsome and rich, we are told – who declares his passionate love for her.

Dorigen tells him she will never be unfaithful to her husband – 'my body is not for auction' – but, to soften the blow, tells Aurelius she will go to bed with him if he can clear the Brittany coast of all its rocks, which are a hazard to shipping. Knowing this is impossible, Aurelius tells her he has no choice left but to die 'a piteous death'. However, he prays to Apollo and Lucina (Juno), the goddess of the moon and childbirth, to cover the coast of Brittany with a flood to cover the rocks.

When this prayer does not work, Aurelius' brother, a clerk, takes him to his former university in Orleans to meet a necromancer (although Chaucer, or the Franklin, is careful to add, 'It is all foolishness to us nowadays, of course, worth less than nothing. The faith of the Holy Church is all we need. We no longer put any trust in magic or necromancy'). The magician uses his knowledge of the moon and stars, the Franklin tells us ('I am no expert in astrology, so bear with me'), to make the rocks disappear.

Appalled, Dorigen resolves to die rather than face 'dishonour and degradation' by giving herself to Aurelius. Her husband has by now returned and – like Dianora's husband in the *Decameron* – tells her she must keep her word. When Dorigen tells this to Aurelius, however, he has a change of heart. He decides to 'forgo his lust [rather] than to perform a wretched deed', and notifies the magician, who forgoes his fee. 'Now, fellow pilgrims,' the Franklin says, 'answer this riddle. Which one of these gentlemen was the most generous?'

Then there is 'The Merchant's Tale', a Chaucerian version of the ninth story on the seventh day in the *Decameron* (*Decameron* 7:9). Both – again – tell of young wives with passionate admirers, and both involve pear trees. Boccaccio's story is told by Panfilo, one of the young men, who begins by telling the ladies in the group that, in his view, 'there is nothing a person who loves passionately will not do, however difficult and uncertain'. Panfilo tells the story of a rich-but-elderly nobleman in ancient Greece called Nicostrato, whose wife, the beautiful, high-spirited, and young Lidia, falls in love with one of his servants, the handsome Pirro. She is 'a fresh young woman', she confides to her maid, but her husband is much too old, and so she is 'badly served in that one thing in which young women take most pleasure'.

The maid tells this to Pirro, who is at first reluctant in case he is being tested – and in case his master finds out – but, in the end, he agrees to be Lidia's lover, provided she kills her husband's favourite falcon in front of him, gives him a lock of her husband's beard, and gives him 'one of his best teeth'. She does all three, dashing the hawk against a wall and pretending to his friends it is an act of revenge for the time her husband spends away from her hunting; playfully pulling hair from his beard; and extracting a supposedly rotten tooth on the grounds that he has bad breath.

Pirro then agrees that Lidia has met his apparently impossible demands. She pretends to be ill, gets Nicostrato and Pirro to carry her into the garden, and asks Pirro to climb up into a pear tree to pick some pears for her. Pirro looks down and pretends he can see the husband and wife making love, which they deny. Pirro then says the pear tree must have the power of optical illusion, and Nicostrato climbs up to see if this is true. When he looks down, he sees Pirro and his wife on the ground making love, and he climbs down in a fury, calling his wife a 'wicked slut', but by the time he reaches the ground the lovers have separated and deny that anything happened. They convince him that the bewitched pear tree must have made him see an illusion, and they have the tree cut down, after which they all return to the palace, where 'many a time thereafter, with greater leisure, Pirro took delight and pleasure of Lidia, and she of him'. How the ladies listening to the story react to this Boccaccio does not tell us, except that they 'lamented the chopping down of the blameless pear tree'.

In the *Canterbury Tales*, Chaucer puts the story not in ancient Greece but – tellingly – in Italy. In 'The Merchant's Tale', a knight in Pavia called January, having been a bachelor for sixty years and having 'enjoyed himself with any number of women', none the less decides to get married. The Merchant, described as a canny trader – good at exchange dealings – with a forked beard, expensive boots, and a Flemish beaver hat, tells the story in Chaucerian fashion – 'I am not making this up' – and begins with his views on women and marriage. A wife is, he says, 'a gift from God' and not, as the Greek philosopher Theophrastus says, a woman who thinks only of her husband's 'goods and chattels' and is bound to be unfaithful to him. No, a wife is for life, and 'can last a long time – longer, perhaps, than you might like'. Wives approve of everything their husbands do, and offer their husbands help and comfort. '"Do this," he says. "Of course, sir," she replies. That is the way it is. Oh happy sacrament of matrimony!'

Now, this January, the Merchant says, had been thinking about acquiring 'the quiet and order of a settled home' and 'the honey pot of a fair wife', and tells his friends he wants to marry a young and pretty woman. They warn him that such a woman will soon tire of him and look for a more vigorous man, but he goes ahead and marries the young May, 'as fresh and lovely as a spring morning … I cannot explain her beauty. Words fail me'. After a wedding feast with 'a hot punch of spice and sweetened wine, as an aphrodisiac', January takes his bride to bed and makes vigorous love to her (or so he thinks), despite his 'scrawny neck and bony face'. But January suddenly goes blind, and it turns out May has an admirer in the house, January's servant Damian, who slips her a love letter in a silk purse. She, in turn, gives him a key to the walled garden, and when her blind husband takes her there one day, Damian climbs up into a pear tree to hide. May persuades

January to bend down so she can climb into the tree, ostensibly to pick pears but in reality to make love to Damian.

Chaucer then introduces classical figures watching this drama: Pluto, described as king of the fairies (rather than the underworld), and Proserpina, his wife. Pluto maintains that all women are frail, fickle, and 'treacherous towards men', to which Proserpina replies that women are true, faithful, and virtuous – and when they are not, they are good at excuses and always win an argument with men, who are 'as gullible as geese'.

To prove his point, when Pluto sees May and Damian making love in the pear tree, he gives January back his sight, and on looking up into the tree the old man sees Damian 'thrusting away'. The narrating Merchant says, 'I will say no more about it. It is not polite.' (Chaucer even apologises to women listeners, or readers: '*Ladyes, I prey yow that ye be nat wrooth; I kan nat glose, I am a rude man*'.) January is furious, calling his wife a whore, but she claims that by managing 'to struggle with a man up a tree', as she had been told to do in a vision, she had cured his blindness, 'as God is my witness'. January is imagining things, May says, adding, 'that is all the thanks I get for curing your blindness' and bursting theatrically into tears.

'Now, wife,' January says, 'let us forget all about it. Come down from the pear tree. If I have slandered you, then I am well punished for it by your tears.' May suggests that he has still not fully recovered his sight and that, in any case, men are fooled every day by their fantasies. 'He who misunderstands, misjudges.' She jumps down into his arms, and they go back to the palace. 'God in heaven!' says Harry Bailly as the Merchant ends his tale. 'Keep me away from a wife like that! Do you realise how many tricks and deceits a woman can use? They are busy as bees, morning and night, trying to fool us.' His own wife, the landlord tells the pilgrims, is a shrew:

> Between you and me, I wish that I were not wed to her. Of course I would be a fool to repeat all of her faults. Do you know why? It would get back to her. There would be gossip by one or two members of this company. I do not need to name names. You all know who I mean. Women have a way about them.

In both Chaucer and the *Decameron*, the young wife is disappointed by her wealthy-but-old husband's sexual performance, and is attracted to a younger and more vigorous man; in both cases, the wife's lover is a trusted servant in her husband's household; and, in both cases, the key to the deception is the pear tree.

Chaucer may also have drawn for his 'Merchant's Tale' on the last story of the second day in the *Decameron* (2:10), told by Dioneo, in which an aged judge in Pisa called Ricciardo di Chinzica marries a young girl called Bartolomea, 'one of the fairest young ladies of Pisa', but is only just about able to consummate his marriage 'by the skin of his teeth'. He then draws up a calendar of saints' days, on which he claims it is sinful to engage in intercourse, as a result of which Bartolomea runs off with a young pirate called Paganino. Ricciardo tracks her down to Monaco, but she tells him she is 'young and lusty', and he should have realised what it is that 'young women need over and above their food and clothing, although modesty prevents them from naming it'. Her husband is clearly 'more assiduous in serving God than in servicing women'. Ricciardo returns to Pisa a broken man and dies there, after which Bartolomea is free to marry Paganino. What is striking, apart from the fact that once again we have a young wife and an aged husband, is the fact that just like old January in Chaucer's tale, Ricciardo needs a drink after his wedding night efforts – in his case Vernaccia, and in old January's case a '*vernage of spices hoote*', a remarkable similarity that suggests more than coincidence.

'The Reeve's Tale' draws on the sixth story on the ninth day of the *Decameron* (9:6), told by Panfilo, which tells of a man who gives food and drink and – 'at a pinch' – a bed to wayfarers at his small house on the River Mugnone just outside Florence. A local young man called Pinuccio is in love with the man's teenage daughter Niccolosa, a 'fine buxom lass', and, together with his friend Adriano, he pretends to be coming back from Romagna and in need of a night's lodging.

The host has only one bedroom, with three beds in it plus a crib for a baby, so he puts Pinuccio and Adriano in one bed; himself and his wife – a 'very handsome woman' – in the second, with the cradle beside it; and his daughter in the third. During the night, Pinuccio goes to the daughter's bed and she, 'though nervous', lets him 'take that pleasure with her which both of them desired'.

Adriano gets up in the night for a 'call of nature', bumps into the crib, and puts it back by his own bed by mistake. The wife, who sleeps naked, gets up in the night when she hears a cat knock something over and, coming back to the bedroom, searches for the crib and so gets into bed with Adriano by mistake (supposedly, at least), and they make love.

Pinuccio then creeps back to what he thinks is the bed he shares with Adriano but gets into bed by mistake with the owner of the house and tells him he has just enjoyed 'the rarest sport' with the delightful Niccolosa. The man is furious, but his wife, realising (belatedly) that she is in bed with Adriano, pretends she has spent the night in her daughter's bed herself, and that her husband must have imagined things: 'You men drink so much of an evening that you do nothing but dream all night and go sleepwalking'. The host laughs, 'mocking Pinuccio and his dreams', and the two young men head back to Florence.

Chaucer's version is told by Oswald the Reeve, an efficient estate manager in Norfolk – 'I dare say that he even managed the worms' – who has amassed a small fortune but is described as skinny and bad tempered, his hair 'shorn around his ears like that of a priest', and is always the last in the line of pilgrims on his sturdy dapple grey horse. The Reeve tells Harry Bailly he cannot tell a lewd story, as the Miller has just done, because he is getting old, with white hair and a frail heart. On the other hand, the Reeve says, old men are still 'tickled by desire'; their strength may have gone, and their 'members may not rise to the occasion', but the longing is still there, and the fire still smoulders in the white ashes. Harry Bailly, impatient with this prologue – 'Do you really want to give us a sermon? … Are you a priest? I don't think so' – urges the Reeve to get on with his story, since 'we are already at Deptford and it is half past seven in the morning'.

The Reeve then tells of a bald, fat miller called Simkin at Trumpington, near Cambridge, who has an 'arrogant and self-important' wife, a 'well proportioned' young daughter, and a baby boy in a cradle. One of the miller's clients is Trinity College Cambridge, and two 'high-spirited and playful' students there, John and Alan (Chaucer gives them Northern dialects), decide to visit the mill to bring some corn and flour back – and to check reports that Simkin has short-changed the college, knowing that the college manciple (steward) is ill. The students – both from a town 'somewhere in the North of England. I have no idea where' – set off on a horse armed with swords – 'these country roads are not always safe' – and arrive at the mill to fill their sack with corn and flour. The crafty miller, however, unties their horse, and while they are looking for it takes half a bushel of flour from the sack to cheat them. By the time they find the horse and return, it is dark, so the miller puts them up in his bedroom along with his wife, his daughter, himself, and the baby in a crib.

After an evening meal with a great deal to drink, they all retire to sleep, with the miller and his wife snoring so loudly – 'God, did they snore. They could have taken the roof off' – that Alan decides it is safe to make love to the daughter: 'She did not say "oh no". Oh no. They were at it in a moment' As in Boccaccio's original, John gets up in the night and moves the crib, so that when the miller's wife also gets up and comes back to the bedroom she feels for the crib and gets into bed with John by mistake, with the inevitable result. 'She had not enjoyed herself so much for years,' we are told ('*so myrie a fit ne hadde she nat ful yoore*').

Towards morning – again, as in the *Decameron* – Alan gets into bed with the miller by mistake, thinking he is John, and tells him he has made love to the daughter three times during the night. The furious miller starts to punch Alan but wakes his wife, who seizes a stick and, not seeing who she is beating, knocks the miller senseless. The two students make a run for it, but not before taking a loaf that, the daughter tells Alan, was made with the flour stolen from their sack.

'That is what happens to deceitful millers,' the Reeve concludes. 'They never learn their lesson.' The Cook, Roger of Ware, who is to tell the next story, sits on his horse with a smile on his face and says, 'The miller certainly got paid back for giving the scholars lodging. He should have known the saying of Solomon: Don't bring every man into your house.'

Then there is the first story on the eighth day of the *Decameron* (8:1), told by Neifile, one of the young ladies, in which she tells of Gulfardo, a German mercenary soldier in Milan, who falls in love (or lust) with Madonna Ambruogia, the wife of the wonderfully named Guasparruolo Cagastraccio, a Milanese merchant. She agrees to grant Gulfardo her favours, provided he keeps their affair secret – and pays her 200 gold florins.

Appalled at this 'sordid behaviour', Gulfardo decides instead to trick the lady, or 'this vile female' as Neifile (or Boccaccio) puts it. He goes to Cagastraccio and asks for a loan of 200 florins at the usual rate of interest. When Cagastraccio goes to Genoa on business, Gulfardo goes to his house and gives Ambruogia the gold coins, asking her to give them to her husband when he returns, a request that she assumes is a cover story for anyone listening.

She then gives Gulfardo 'full satisfaction of her body' that night, and 'on many other nights' until Cagastraccio returns – at which point, Gulfardo tells the merchant he is returning the 200 florins he borrowed because the deal he meant them for has fallen through, and has given them to his wife. Ambruogia is then obliged to hand the money to her husband, and Gulfardo has thus 'enjoyed his grasping mistress without any cost to himself'. The young men and ladies listening to the story agree the 'greedy Milanese lady' has been justly punished.

In 'The Shipman's Tale', Chaucer sets the story in Saint-Denis, near Paris. The Shipman, or captain, who comes from Dartmouth and has navigated his ship, the *Magdalene*, to Carthage, Finisterre, and 'every creek in Brittany and Spain', tells the story of a merchant called Peter and his beautiful wife, who is admired by Peter's bosom pal, a 'good-looking, fresh-faced and virile' thirty-year-old monk from Paris called John.

When Peter announces he is going away to Bruges on business, his wife complains to John that, although a woman wants her husband to be healthy, wealthy, wise, and generous, as well as obedient and good in bed, Peter 'isn't worth as much as a fly'. Above all, he is stingy, and she needs 100 francs to pay for her new gowns. Before Peter sets off for Flanders, John asks for a loan of 100 francs 'to purchase some cattle for the monastery'. The moment Peter is gone, John the monk presents himself to the wife, freshly shaven and with his tonsure neatly clipped, gives her the 100 francs, and they go to bed:

'She promised she would give him value for money; and so she did, throughout the night.'

When Peter returns, John tells him he has returned the 100 francs – to his wife. She admits to her husband that John gave her the money, but she claims she has spent it 'on fine clothes and on hospitality' and 'not a penny has been wasted'. Peter forgives her but asks her to, in future, 'try not to overspend. Keep your money in your purse'. 'Well spoken, Shipman,' says Harry Bailly. 'May you sail around the coasts for ever and a day, master mariner! But may that false monk, cousin John, have nothing but bad luck for the rest of his life!'

'The Shipman's Tale' also draws on the next story in the *Decameron*, 8:2, in which a priest gives a farm labourer's 'jolly and buxom' wife his cloak so she will go to bed with him, but later claims it back from her husband on the grounds he had only lent it. There may be an echo, too, of *Decameron* 8:10, in which a Florentine cloth merchant gives 500 gold florins to a Sicilian lady in Palermo so she will go to bed with him, but later uses a ruse to trick her into giving him back three times as much.

Similarities may be noted, too, between Chaucer's 'Miller's Tale' and the fourth story on the third day of the *Decameron* (3:4). In the *Decameron* story, a cuckolded husband stands on the roof with his arms stretched out 'like a crucifix' to gain sainthood while his wife and her lover enjoy themselves in the rooms below; 'The Miller's Tale' involves tubs hung from the roof in which the husband, John, is persuaded by a student called Nicholas to spend the night to avoid a recurrence of Noah's Flood, so that Nicholas can go to bed with John's wife,

Alison. In both stories, the lovers use religion to get women into bed, and in both the lovers enjoy the women practically in the presence of their husbands.

Peter Beidler comments:

> [The *Decameron*] was written by the man from whom Chaucer borrowed more than he borrowed from any other writer, and he might well have availed himself of a copy on one of his diplomatic journeys to Italy; Chaucer fails to mention many of his sources, such as Boccaccio's *Teseida*, his acknowledged source for 'The Knight's Tale', or Boccaccio's *Filostrato*, his source for *Troilus and Criseyde,* and so we should not attach any particular significance to his failure to mention Boccaccio's *Decameron*.

'Just Say Yes, Chaucer Knew the *Decameron*' is the no-nonsense title of Beidler's essay in a 2000 edition of *The Decameron and the Canterbury Tales.* Or, as John Tatlock put it in 1966:

> In view of his several months of sojourn and travel in Italy, including a visit to Florence, and in view of his taste for reading and inexhaustible curiosity, it is incredible that he had not heard of the *Decameron,* and indeed seen it. If he never bought a copy, that may have been because it was a very large and expensive book and he was not an affluent man.

10

The Mission to Lombardy

By the time of Chaucer's next visit to Italy, in 1378, he was becoming known as a writer, but he was still very much a diplomat and court official: in 1374, the year after his visit to Genoa and Florence, he had been appointed comptroller of customs for wools, skins, and tanned hides, an important – and demanding – post involving detailed management of the highly profitable wool trade and the shady dealing it often involved. People in the Middle Ages were seen as divided into 'those who fight, those who pray, and those who work' – a phrase coined by John of Worcester, a twelfth-century monk and chronicler. Chaucer undoubtedly both fought and prayed, but what he mainly did was work.

The Custom House was situated on Wool Quay in Thames Street, where Chaucer had grown up, so it was in an area – and trade – with which Chaucer was thoroughly familiar. The Custom House was some ten minutes' walk from Aldgate and just upstream of the Tower of London. At the time of writing, there are plans to turn the Custom House – much expanded and rebuilt since the Middle Ages, and until recently an office of HM Revenue and Customs – into a riverside hotel.

Chaucer was by now in his mid-thirties, and although he had written the *Book of the Duchess* and translated the courtly love poem *Roman de la Rose* from the French, most of his output as an author – including the *Canterbury Tales* – was yet to come. On the other hand, his job at Custom House would have kept him in contact with the land and culture of Petrarch and Boccaccio, since Italian merchants played a prominent role in the wool trade and Italian bankers financed it. Italians were therefore a common sight (and sound) in London, and in East Anglia and the Cotswolds, where historic 'wool churches' – churches that were financed primarily by donated profits from the wool market – still testify to the trade that once sustained them. English wool was the mainstay of the English economy in the Middle Ages: it was exported to Italy, France, and the Low Countries, the centres of the emerging cloth-making industries – and its revenues and taxes financed Edward III's military campaigns.

Chaucer makes no mention of his post as comptroller in his writings, unlike his friend and fellow poet John Gower, who wrote scathing satires about the wool trade. But then, as Eileen Power noted in her landmark Ford Lecture in 1939, *The Wool Trade in English Medieval History*, the English nation was 'intensely wool conscious' from 'king to peasant', and 'if Chaucer is silent on the subject it is probably because as a customs officer he saw too much of it in his working hours'.

Another likely reason for his silence was the corruption and underhand dealing that went on in the wool trade. Gower may have been scathing about the wheeler-dealing in the wool business, but Chaucer 'kept his head down', as Paul Strohm puts it. Duties paid on wool exports amounted to over one-third of the total income of the realm. Strohm writes:

> In the honest part of the business, wool was conscientiously weighed and duties collected and passed on to the royal exchequer. Any honest trading that might occur was far overshadowed, however, by an invisible wool economy based on dishonest skimming, false weighing, and other forms of smuggling and illicit profit-taking.

Wool merchants and dealers in London were the wealthy oligarchs of their day, and collectors of the wool custom could – and did – 'take bribes, enhance profits by weighing wet wool, favour friends, ship their own unauthorised cargoes, and engage in other profit-making scams'. The comptroller of customs was supposed to supervise the wool trade and ensure that such abuses did not happen, and had charge of the 'cocket', or seal, confirming shipments as legitimate, but was often – like Chaucer – less powerful and connected than the men he was meant to control.

On the other hand, Chaucer had clearly not enriched himself in the job, since by the time he stepped down he was in debt. Chaucer survived twelve years in the job, and was evidently judged a success, since in 1382 he was given an additional job as comptroller of export and import duties on wine and other merchandise – a reflection, no doubt, of his family's trade. But in 1386 Parliament demanded the dismissal of long-serving comptrollers, 'because they perpetuate great oppressions and extortions against the people'.

When he was appointed comptroller, Chaucer had been granted a lease on an apartment – presumably rent-free, since no payment is mentioned – above Aldgate in the City of London 'for the whole life of him the said Geoffrey', with additional use of a cellar. The apartment was close to the Custom House; he was to keep it in good repair, and not sublet it.

There is no mention in the lease of his wife, Philippa, suggesting that he lodged there on his own, conveniently close to his place of work, while she perhaps lived with John of Gaunt and his second wife, Constance of Castile, at Tutbury Castle in Staffordshire (now a ruin), which was a seat of the Earls of Lancaster. Philippa's sister, after all, was Gaunt's mistress (and later his third wife), Katherine Swynford. Little is known about Chaucer's marriage: Samantha Katz Seal has accused some male historians of depicting Philippa as either 'a harpy or harlot' or a shrewish and cold careerist, or both, on the basis of little or no evidence. There has been speculation that she was another of Gaunt's many mistresses, but of that there is no proof either.

Chaucer later had to give up the Aldgate lodgings when he ceased to be comptroller, despite the supposed lease for life, but seems to have still been given 'a gallon pitcher of wine daily', which was also 'for life'. The fortified and crenellated Aldgate tower had existed as a defensive structure since Roman times. Rebuilt in the twelfth and thirteenth centuries, it was given a portcullis and chains in 1377, three years after Chaucer started to take up residence there. The city gate was closed at night and opened again in the early morning. It was taken down in the eighteenth century, but a water pump survives at the junction of Leadenhall Street and Fenchurch Street, and although the present pump is a now-defunct Victorian adaptation, it is where Chaucer would have drawn his water.

It was in his Aldgate lodging that Chaucer did his writing, despite the noise from the busy street below: in addition to the carts, traders, travellers, and street cries, two nearby churches – St Katharine Cree and St Botolph's (both rebuilt in later years, but both still there) – had powerful bells. So, too, did All Hallows by the Tower, which belonged to Barking Abbey and was frequented by Genoese merchants who moored their ships at a nearby quay, and the now-vanished Holy Trinity Priory at Aldgate (a further victim of Henry VIII; none of its buildings remain). As Tim Machan reminds us, we have to picture Chaucer writing away – despite the noise – on a quire, 'a stack of perhaps four parchment sheets folded in half to make eight leaves and sixteen writing pages'. In the *House of Fame*, the talking eagle – who flies Chaucer through the air, as the eagle carries Dante in the *Divine Comedy* – upbraids Chaucer for going home and 'sitting at another book' instead of enjoying '*rest and newe thynges*' after a busy day at work doing '*alle thy rekenynges*'. Chaucer had a demanding working life supervising the wool and wine trades (his 'reckonings'), yet he seems to have been one of those writers who was most productive when he was busy with other matters.

Above all, Chaucer had to adapt to a change of monarch: in 1377, after a reign of fifty years, Edward III died, and the crown passed to his grandson Richard II, the son of Edward, the Black Prince. As we have seen, Edward III's reign had

at first been marked by successes in the wars with France –
now known as the Hundred Years' War – including the Battle
of Crecy in 1346, the conquest of Calais the following year,
and the Battle of Poitiers in 1356, won by the Black Prince
despite the fact that his forces were outnumbered. But in
1376 the Black Prince suddenly died of dysentery, which he
had contracted in Spain, and, as was recorded in Chapter
2, another son, Lionel of Antwerp, had died at Alba in 1368
shortly after his wedding in Milan to Violante Visconti.
Edward III himself suffered from poor health, increasingly
relying on his chancellor, William Wykeham, and on his mistress, Alice Perrers, former lady-in-waiting to Queen Philippa,
who had died of dropsy – the swelling of fluid in the tissues
that we now call oedema – in 1369.

Alice, who was later banished from the court because of
her excessive influence and outspoken manner, is sometimes
suggested to have been one of the inspirations behind the
no-nonsense Alison, the Wife of Bath. The royal mistress
was certainly a colourful character, who in 1375 rode from
the Tower of London to Smithfield dressed as the so-called
Lady of the Sun. As Haldeen Braddy has noted, a number of
her friends and supporters were also close to Chaucer, including Philip de la Vache, Lewis Clifford, and two officials who
went with Chaucer on his missions abroad: Guichard d'Angle
and Richard Stury. Alice may even have been responsible for
Chaucer getting his apartment at Aldgate, where she also held
property. For the medieval chronicler Thomas of Walsingham,
on the other hand, Alice was a 'shameless, impudent harlot' of
low birth, who, though 'not beautiful', had a seductive voice.

Before turning her charms on Edward III, she had been the mistress of 'a man of Lombardy', Thomas tells us, though unfortunately he does not say who her alleged Italian lover was.

Richard II, the new monarch, was only ten years old. The kingdom was therefore, in reality, run in Richard's early years by his uncles, two surviving sons of Edward III and Philippa of Hainault: Chaucer's future brother-in-law, the powerful John of Gaunt, and, to a lesser extent, Thomas of Woodstock, the Duke of Gloucester. When it came to European diplomacy, Chaucer was evidently as useful to the young Richard II – and to John of Gaunt – as he had been to the elderly Edward, making several trips to Europe 'on the king's secret business'.

The purposes of voyages Chaucer is known to have made to France and Flanders in 1376–7 are unclear; some historians suggest he was sent on a mission, with Jean Froissart, to arrange a marriage between the teenage Richard and a French princess, thereby ending the Hundred Years' War. The trip to Lombardy in 1378 may have had a similar purpose, namely a marriage between Richard II and Caterina, one of the daughters of Bernabò Visconti. No such weddings occurred, however: in the end, Richard II married Anne of Bohemia, daughter of Holy Roman Emperor Charles IV, in 1382. In other respects, Chaucer's journey to Lombardy is well documented. On 10 May 1378, Richard II despatched Edward de Berkeley and Chaucer as envoys to Lombardy to meet '*Barnabo dominum de Mellan*' (Bernabò Visconti, lord of Milan) and '*Johannem de Haukewode*' (John Hawkwood, the English-born condottiere and legendary mercenary head of the White Company), '*pro certis negociis expedicionem guerre Regis tangentibus*' ('on certain affairs touching the expedition of the king's wars'). Hawkwood had married Visconti's daughter Donnina and was therefore Visconti's son-in-law – and, as we shall see, it was Hawkwood on whom Chaucer at least partly based his character the Knight in the *Canterbury Tales*.

Chaucer set off for Milan on 28 May 1378 '*de civitate Londonie*' and returned to London on 19 September. His knowledge of the Italian language, his likely involvement in the 1368 Milan Visconti wedding, and his previous trip to Italy in 1373 meant that he was clearly considered the man to deal with matters Italian, far more than the leader of the mission, Edward de Berkeley, one of the 'chamber knights' or 'knights of the body' who were close to the king in his household and attended to his daily needs.

From the accounts for the voyage, for which he was given a rate per day, we know Chaucer was away from London for 115 days. De Berkeley was accompanied by nine mounted men and was paid 20 shillings per day, while Chaucer was accompanied by five men and their horses and was paid 13 shillings and 4 pence per day, exactly two-thirds as much as de Berkeley. The mission to Milan therefore involved a group of sixteen men, with Chaucer as the deputy leader, though with an entourage in his own right.

Over the previous two years, as we have seen, Chaucer had been on official journeys to Flanders and Paris, and he was very much still a court diplomat as well as comptroller at the Custom House, where a deputy, Richard Barret (or Baret) was appointed to carry out Chaucer's work while he was away in

Italy. In a sign that controlling the wool trade could sometimes be a risky business, Chaucer also gave power of attorney to his fellow poet John Gower and another close friend called Richard Forrester, so that they could represent him if a lawsuit were brought against him while he was abroad.

Almost certainly, Chaucer and de Berkeley followed the well-worn route to Italy, crossing the Channel and then following the Rhine and crossing the Alps into Lombardy, and taking a month to complete the 1,200-km journey to Milan. Chaucer therefore arrived as Italy was basking in the heat and light of summer, probably at the end of June – a contrast with his 1372–3 journey, in which he would have crossed the Alps in icy winter conditions.

He arrived at a critical time both for the Church and the Visconti family. The Church was gripped by growing signs of the Western Schism in the Catholic Church, with rival popes vying for the loyalty of the faithful. By the time Chaucer was born, popes had been based in Avignon rather than Rome for over thirty years, so he must have seen it as the norm. Following a dispute between the papacy and the French Crown, no fewer than seven popes had resided in Avignon from 1309 to 1376, in the magnificent Palais des Papes, which still dominates Avignon's centre. Pope Gregory XI, the last of the Avignon popes, had eventually returned the papacy and the Curia back to Rome in 1377, even though he was himself French. When he died a year later, in March 1378 – just before Chaucer and de Berkeley set off for Italy – he was succeeded by an Italian, Bartolomeo Prignano, archbishop of Bari since 1377, who in April 1378 took the title Pope Urban VI.

During the Avignon period, powerful local families in Italy had taken full advantage of the absence of the popes to establish themselves in nominally papal cities including Bologna, Rimini, Forli, and Faenza. Even in Rome itself, the Orsini and Colonna families vied for supremacy. But Egidio Albornoz, a Spanish cardinal and the former archbishop of Toledo, was sent to Italy to re-establish papal control, with the help of mercenaries such as the White Company. By the time of Urban VI's election, Albornoz and the White Company had secured sufficient papal control for a return of the Curia to Rome to be plausible. It was at first thought that Urban VI would be acceptable to the French cardinals, since he had trained at Avignon. But the influential French cardinals at the conclave quickly came to regret the decision to elect him and withdrew from Rome to Anagni. It did not help, perhaps, that Urban VI's real power base was not Rome but Naples, and that he was considered to lack 'Christian gentleness and charity'. On 2 August, while Chaucer was in Lombardy, the French cardinals unilaterally pronounced the election of Urban VI null and void, and shortly afterwards they elected a rival pope, Robert of Geneva, archbishop of Cambrai in northern France. He took the title Clement VII and returned the papacy to Avignon. Since the Italian cardinals still supported Urban VI as pope, there were now two rival pontiffs.

Then there was the upheaval in the Visconti family – not, perhaps, as cataclysmic as the split in the Church, but for Chaucer no less important, and perhaps even more so, since he was intimately involved with the Viscontis following the short-lived wedding between Galeazzo II Visconti's daughter,

Violante, and Edward III's son Lionel ten years before. On 4 August, while Chaucer was still in Lombardy, Galeazzo II died at Pavia, which he had made his power base, leaving Bernabò in sole charge. It is highly likely that Chaucer went to Pavia either to see Galeazzo II before he died or to mourn his death; Pavia is less than 50 km from Milan. Galeazzo II had been closely associated with Petrarch and had constructed a great library in his fortress at Pavia, where the University of Pavia had been founded by Holy Roman Emperor Charles IV in 1361. More immediately, Galeazzo II's death created a vacuum in Lombardy that his brother Bernabò now filled, and the rise of Bernabò to supreme power in Milan was linked to the schism in the Church. Although Milan was – like Florence – a Guelph state, in theory favouring the pope rather than the Holy Roman Emperor, the Viscontis had increasingly fallen out with Rome, not least over their loss of control over Bologna to the Papal States in 1360.

John Hawkwood had initially put his mercenary forces at the disposal of Rome, but – as ever – he was willing to switch sides if paid enough. Florence duly offered Hawkwood 130,000 florins, plus a pension for life of 1,200 florins a year and an annual salary of 600 florins. That did the trick, and Florence and Milan then joined forces to foment unrest in the Papal States, including Bologna and Perugia and – uncomfortably close to Rome – Orvieto and Viterbo. The resulting conflict came to be known as the War of the Eight Saints (*Otto Santi*), though this appears to be an ironic reference not to actual saints but to the eight members of Florence's ruling body, the Signoria. It lasted three years, and only ended when a peace treaty was negotiated with Pope Urban VI at Tivoli, just 30 km from Rome, in July 1378 – the very period when Chaucer and de Berkeley were in Italy.

There is no proof that they were at the talks in Tivoli, a Guelph commune that supported Urban VI against Clement VII, the 'antipope' in Avignon, but they may well have been – and, in any case, they must have been involved in the attempts to resolve the conflict. As the literary scholar Ernest Kuhl put it in an article entitled 'Why was Chaucer sent to Milan in 1378?', 'All evidence points to a momentous mission, one involving a crisis in the history of Western civilisation, involving in fact the very fate of England itself.' Pope Gregory XI had died just forty-four days before, 'time enough for the important news to reach London', and his death, 'which would inevitably affect the outcome of the Hundred Years' War, was the reason why Chaucer was sent to Milan'. And, in dealing with 'certain affairs touching the expedition of the King's wars', Chaucer was negotiating with a man who clearly had made a lasting impression on him when he later came to compose 'The Knight's Tale': John Hawkwood.

11

A *Parfit Gentil Knyght*?

Chaucer had probably first met the famous condottiere John Hawkwood during the Milan wedding or its aftermath in 1368. But the 1378 mission was different: this was not a royal social occasion but rather a complex diplomatic and military tangle, which Chaucer had to try to help unravel – and in which Hawkwood was a key player.

Hawkwood had begun his military career in France, as a longbowman in the Hundred Years' War. The young Hawkwood fought at Crecy in 1346 and at Poitiers in 1356, but in 1361 he became a so-called soldier of fortune, crossing into Italy with a group of mercenaries known as the White Company and rising to become its commander two years later. He was, in effect, a sword for hire, fighting variously for the popes, Pisa, the Viscontis, and Florence: 'condottiere' literally means 'contractor', from '*condotta*' ('contract'). For Italians, his surname was unpronounceable, there being no 'h' in the Italian alphabet; he sometimes referred to himself as 'Haukevvod', perhaps in the hope that this would be easier for Italians to cope with, but he became known in Italy as Giovanni Acuto or Johannes Acutus, meaning literally John

Sharp or John the Astute. Other recorded forms are Aucgunctur, Haughd, Hauvod, Hankelvode, Augudh, Auchevud, Haukevvod, Haukwode, and Haucod.

His exploits gave him almost mythical status in both Italy and England. We cannot be sure what he looked like: the fresco portrait of him on horseback above his tomb in the duomo in Florence, seen by millions of tourists every year, was made by Paolo Uccello in 1436, over forty years after Hawkwood's death. The Florentine chronicler Filippo Villani claimed – picturesquely – that his surname was Hawkwood because his mother gave birth in a forest. In reality, Hawkwood was born about 1320 at Sible Hedingham, in Essex, the second son of Gilbert Hawkwood, a gentleman and landowner of considerable wealth, with property in the Braintree area at both Sible Hedingham and the picturesque village of Finchingfield. It was a time of hardship and famine, but Gilbert Hawkwood was relatively well off and benefited from close links to the local lords, the de Vere family at Castle Hedingham.

It was under John de Vere at Crecy and again at Poitiers that the young John Hawkwood served when Edward III launched his campaign to gain the French throne. His subsequent career as a mercenary in Italy brought him great wealth: whereas the average wage for a craftsman in Florence was 30 florins a year, Hawkwood was earning 6,000 florins a year in the first stage of his career and an unimaginable 80,000 florins by the end.

Hawkwood married twice. His daughter (by his first wife), Antiochia, about whom little is known (she may have been a de Vere), married into a prominent Essex family, the Coggeshalls. His second marriage is better documented: in 1377, when he was about fifty-three, he married Donnina Visconti, the seventeen-year-old daughter of the Milanese ruler Bernabò Visconti by one of Bernabò's many mistresses, Montanina de Lazzari, thus becoming Bernabò's son-in-law – though, as we shall see, they later fell out. Hawkwood and Donnina Visconti had four children and gave them English names: Janet, Catherine, Anna, and John. Like Bernabò Visconti – and many other powerful men of his time – Hawkwood also had many mistresses and illegitimate children.

There is no clear evidence of why he was knighted, or when: some historians suggest he was knighted by the Black Prince after the Battle of Poitiers, but just as likely is that he was simply given the title 'Sir' by the Italians, since in Italy all mercenary army commanders were classified as knights. The White Company took shape in France after the Treaty of Bretigny near Chartres on 8 May 1360, when, as we have seen, Edward III signed a peace deal with France. It was originally called the Great Company but was renamed the White Company because of the white flags its troops carried.

The peace suddenly made Edward III's troops redundant, and Hawkwood signed up to join the mercenaries. Under the Treaty of Bretigny, Edward gave up his claim to the French throne but retained a number of his French possessions, including Aquitaine; John II of France had been obliged to pay a huge ransom for his release and tried to raise funds for it by increasing taxes. On learning that a large amount of this tax revenue was heading for Provence, the White Company decided to take control of Pont-Saint-Esprit, a town on a bridge over the Rhone near Avignon, for three months at the start of 1361. The royal commissioners carrying John II's ransom money heard of the town's capture and evaded the trap. But the White Company none the less robbed Pont-Saint-Esprit and its inhabitants of all the town's goods and cash, and this undoubtedly caused its reputation as a formidable – if unscrupulous – force to spread rapidly, its ranks increasing after Pont-Saint-Esprit to a remarkable 12,000 armed men.

Hawkwood swiftly rose to become the commander of the White Company. The capture of Pont-Saint-Esprit meant the mercenaries could now blockade Avignon itself. Pope Innocent VI wrote a letter from the besieged Palais des Papes to the White Company seeking peace, in a letter that clearly identifies Hawkwood as its leader. The company at first failed to respond to the pope's plea, and its members – including Hawkwood – were excommunicated. But Avignon was suffering from the plague, and the mercenaries lacked food and other supplies, so in March 1361 the White Company struck a deal with the pope that contracted it to fight for him across the Pyrenees in Spain and across the Alps in Italy.

The pope first authorised the mercenaries to join the marquis of Montferrat in his war against Amadeus VI, the ruling count of Savoy, a once-powerful territory in the Western Alps that is now divided between France, Italy, and Switzerland. Together, they successfully attacked Savigliano (in the province of Cuneo) and Rivarolo (in Turin) and remained in Savoy territory for a year. Amadeus VI made his last stand at Lanzo, near Turin, in 1362, leading the marquis of Montferrat to sign a contract with the White Company in November to support him in his next campaign, this time against the Viscontis in Milan.

The war between Pisa and Florence two years later was not such a success for Hawkwood, who headed the Pisan forces but lost the Battle of Cascina in July 1364 on the River Arno between Pisa and Florence, an encounter later chosen by Michelangelo as the subject for an uncompleted mural in the Palazzo Vecchio in Florence (only copies of preparatory drawings survive). At Cascina, Hawkwood knew he was outnumbered and so launched a surprise attack, but he was outmanoeuvred by the rival Florentine commander, Galeotto Malatesta, who took some 2,000 Pisan troops prisoner. Hawkwood and his surviving troops were forced to take refuge in the nearby Abbey of San Savino (of which the church survives today).

The second telling battle in Hawkwood's career was more successful: he had by now abandoned the pope and was employed by Bernabò Visconti in Milan, five years before his daughter Donnina became Hawkwood's wife. Together with Milanese forces, forming the Army of St George, Hawkwood and his men ransacked Siena and surrounding lands including Buonconvento, Roccastrada, and perhaps most famously – or most infamously – the Cistercian Abbey of San Galgano. At San Galgano, they looted all the abbey's holy treasures – though not the celebrated 'sword in the stone', a sword with symbolic Arthurian echoes that Galgano Guidotti, a twelfth-century nobleman-turned-hermit (and later saint) is said to have plunged into the rock to show his family he had renounced all military and worldly matters. Thanks to Hawkwood, the abbey is now roofless and in ruins, though the splendid walls and *rotonda* chapel – and the sword in the stone – survive.

At the Battle of Rubiera in June 1372, fought between papal forces and Bernabò Visconti on the Via Emilia, about 50 km from Bologna, Hawkwood and Visconti outflanked the enemy and captured a number of papal officers. Hawkwood was by now adept, however, at playing one side against another and at demanding – and receiving – bribes to either switch sides or remain neutral. After Rubiera, he marched his forces along the Via Emilia towards the city of Florence, which paid him 130,000 florins to observe a truce, an example then followed by Pisa, Siena, and Arezzo (which also paid Hawkwood not to attack).

Because it was widely believed that Hawkwood was carrying out these raids, or threats of raids, on behalf of Pope Gregory XI, it was at this point that Milan and Florence decided to bury their differences and form an alliance. Siena, Pisa, Lucca, and Arezzo followed suit, as did Queen Joanna I of Naples, the result being a broad Italian defensive league against the pope – and the White Company.

The result was the War of the Eight Saints, starting in 1375, with Hawkwood and his company fighting for Pope Gregory XI against Florence, even though Hawkwood was frequently angered by the pope's failure to pay him the agreed amounts. In December, Hawkwood went to Citta di Castello to put down a rebellion but ended up capturing the city, which was not what the pope had intended – but Hawkwood did so in a (successful) attempt to extract further payment from Gregory XI.

After capturing Citta di Castello, Hawkwood rode in

February 1376 to the Guelph – that is, pro-pope – town of Faenza, where the papal governor was asking for protection because he feared a revolt was brewing. While at Faenza, Hawkwood attempted to lay siege to the neighbouring town of Granarola, but was forced to retreat back to Faenza. There, the papal governor opened the gates to Hawkwood, who, once he had entered, demanded that the inhabitants surrender their arms – and then proceeded to sack the town, since the pope had still not paid him. On hearing of this, Florence bribed Hawkwood not to fight and offered him a pension, as well as forgiveness for all betrayals and wrongdoings that he had committed against Florence. Yet Hawkwood, at this point, still remained with the pope and even took part in the infamous massacre at Cesena, near Rimini on the Adriatic coast, in February 1377. A papal decree had promised forgiveness for citizens of Cesena who laid down their arms, but, in fact, once they had done so, the unarmed civilians were slaughtered on the orders of the pope's representative, Cardinal Robert of Geneva – the future antipope in Avignon (as Clement VII). Three days of rape and killing led to thousands of deaths, with many people drowning in the town moat as they tried to escape.

This was too much even for Hawkwood, and it became a turning point in his career: he now left the papal service altogether and began working for Milan, Florence, and their allies. It was at this critical point that Chaucer and de Berkeley entered the scene, just as the Papal States were losing Hawkwood's support. The three-year War of the Eight Saints finally ended with the peace treaty negotiated with Gregory XI's successor, Pope Urban VI, at Tivoli, near Rome, in July 1378.

Petrarch wrote to Urban VI that his priority as pontiff must now be to restore the church's authority in Rome: 'Correct her ways, relieve her feebleness, curb her avarice, drive away her ambition, restore her lost and rejected sobriety, halt her overflowing lust, prod her listless sluggishness, quell her raging anger.' Chaucer and his English diplomatic mission no doubt played a key role in the treaty negotiations and approved Hawkwood's alliance with Florence and Milan. The Milan–Florence alliance held for several years but did not last: although Hawkwood was Bernabò Visconti's son-in-law, he fell out with him and signed a contract with Florence alone, as a result of which Visconti stripped Hawkwood of the Milanese land he had received in his wife's dowry.

But Hawkwood had landholdings in Italy and England, and by 1385 he was over sixty years old. He had one last campaign to fight: in the winter of 1385–6, war broke out between Padua and Verona, culminating in the Battle of Castagnaro in the Veneto in 1387, often described as Hawkwood's greatest victory. With his cavalry and archers, Hawkwood outflanked the Veronese forces, allegedly by using a fake standard to mislead them about his whereabouts, thus securing victory for himself and his Paduan allies.

Hawkwood died in Florence on 17 March 1394 from a '*subito accidente*' ('sudden accident'), perhaps a heart attack. His funeral three days later was followed by an elaborate memorial service in the Florence duomo, with the city fathers providing three banners with the arms of Florence, and a helmet with a golden lion holding a lily in its claw as the crest. The White Company sent fourteen caparisoned (decorated with ornamental cloth coverings) warhorses, 'bearing the Englishman's personal banner, sword, shield, and helmet', according to a chronicle of the time.

After Hawkwood's death, most of his great wealth disappeared: Donnina travelled to England from Milan to claim the land he owned, only to find out most of the land registers had disappeared due to the plague, making it impossible to prove ownership. The new English king, Richard II, wanted Hawkwood's cremated remains transferred back to his 'native land', but as far as we know they stayed in Florence, where they had already been interred.

There had been intentions to build a marble tomb in the duomo for Hawkwood, but the money was lacking. In 1436, over forty years after Hawkwood's death, the Medici rulers of Florence hired the artist Paolo Uccello to decorate the duomo, and Uccello painted a portrait of Hawkwood that survives today in the third bay of the northern wall. He is seen on a horse, with a commander's baton, dressed in partial armour. Uccello used a technique called *terra verde* to attempt to emulate a bronze statue in painting. The Latin inscription reads, '*Ioannes Acutus eques brittanicus dux aetatis suae cautissimus et rei militaris peritissimus habitus est*' ('John Hawkwood, British knight, most prudent leader of his age and most expert in the art of war').

Hawkwood is also honoured at St Peter's Church at Sible Hedingham: most of his decorated tomb there has disappeared, but a canopied arch bears symbolic pictures of a hawk, a boar, and a pelican. The altar once had an image of Hawkwood standing in prayer, with Hawkwood saying,

'Son of God, remember me,' his first wife saying, 'Mother of mine, remember me,' and his second wife saying, 'Mother of Christ, remember me.' It is possible that when Donnina came to England to claim Hawkwood's Essex properties she brought his heart with her, since it was common at the time to bury the body parts of a famous person separately.

Exactly where Chaucer met Hawkwood is not recorded: Robert Pratt has pointed out that in the summer of 1378 Hawkwood's company was besieging Verona on behalf of Bernabò Visconti of Milan, whose wife, Beatrice Regina, was from the della Scala family, known as the Scaligeri, which ruled Verona in the Middle Ages. Their elaborate tombs can still be seen at Verona's Romanesque church of Santa Maria Antica, which was in effect the della Scala private chapel. Beatrice, the 'Lady of Milan', gave her name to the church of Santa Maria alla Scala, which in the eighteenth century was demolished to make way for La Scala Opera House on the same site.

Hawkwood approached Verona through a narrow corridor between Lake Garda and Mantua, and during Chaucer's visit Hawkwood's camp was at Monzambano in the valley of the River Mincio, 10 km south of Lake Garda and 25 km north of Mantua. Verona was 25 km to the east, but Hawkwood kept raiding and pillaging Mantuan land despite protests from Ludovico Gonzaga, the Mantua marchese. We know this because of letters Hawkwood and his officers John Thornbury and William Gold wrote to Gonzaga, now kept in the Mantua state archive. Chaucer could have met Hawkwood, therefore, near Mantua and Lake Garda. The archives also show, however, that Hawkwood was often in Milan, as of course was Bernabò Visconti, so it is equally possible that it was in Milan itself that Hawkwood met Chaucer and de Berkeley, most likely at Bernabò's castle near the Porta Romana.

Hawkwood is seen by some as the model for Chaucer's *parfit gentil knyght*, a man full of chivalry, truth, honour, generosity, and courtesy ('*gentil*' meaning 'genteel' or 'noble' rather than 'gentle'). Arthur Conan Doyle's 1891 novel *The White Company* depicts the fourteenth century as an age of chivalry and gallantry. In reality, Hawkwood's troops dismembered their enemies, raped women, and murdered unarmed peasants, and Hawkwood himself was responsible for a number of atrocities including the massacre at Cesena. The German nineteenth-century medieval historian Ferdinand Gregorovius found it ironic that Florence had denied Dante, its greatest citizen, a final resting place in the city, yet had afforded a place of honour to 'that robber of a Hawkwood'. The nickname Giovanni Acuto, William Caferro suggests in his biography, 'points to Hawkwood's most prominent characteristic in the eyes of his Italian contemporaries – his cleverness and cunning'. On the other hand, all forces in the Middle Ages were ruthless, and Chaucer's Knight, we learn in the prologue to the *Canterbury Tales*, had 'done nobly in his sovereign's war and ridden into battle, no man more, as well in Christian as in heathen places, and ever honoured for his noble graces'. Hawkwood's contemporaries would surely have recognised that description as applying to him. The inscription on his memorial in Florence reads that he was the 'most prudent' and 'most expert' general of his time. Terry Jones has suggested in *Chaucer's Knight: The Portrait of a Medieval Mercenary* that the Knight in 'The Knight's Tale' is based on Hawkwood and that Chaucer knew from personal experience the realities of war, having known Hawkwood and having fought in battle at Reims himself as a young man.

Chaucer would have known Ramon Llull's *Book of the Order of Chivalry*, written a hundred years earlier in the late thirteenth century as a treatise on the duties of the 'perfect knight' and encouraging 'loyalty, truth, courage, generosity, decency, humility, and pity' as chivalric virtues along with 'sense and discretion'. Chaucer may also have drawn on Nicholas Sabraham, whom he certainly met through Hawkwood and whose travels as a Crusader mirror more closely those of the fictional Knight, involving Scotland, France, Spain, Prussia, Hungary, Greece, Turkey, and Alexandria (and not Italy, significantly).

In 1385–6, Sabraham gave evidence in the dispute between Richard Scrope and Robert Grosvenor in the Court of Chivalry over which of them had the right to the *azure, a bend or* coat of arms, as did Chaucer – and, like Chaucer, Sabraham supported Scrope, saying he had seen Scrope with the coat of arms in Scotland, Prussia, Hungary, and Constantinople, whereas he had 'never heard of Sir Robert Grosvenor or his ancestors'. Sabraham testified that he had also seen the burial place of a Scrope in a church at Mesembria – now Nesebar in Bulgaria – on the Black Sea coast, and that, too, had the said coat of arms on a wall above it.

The Knight who draws the short straw at the start of the *Canterbury Tales* and is therefore asked by Harry Bailly to tell his fellow pilgrims the first story – the tale of Palamon, Arcite, and Emily – may well reflect Hawkwood, Sabraham, and other knights whom Chaucer had known personally. The tale the Knight tells, however, comes from Boccaccio's *Teseida* – and the 1378 mission to Lombardy almost certainly gave Chaucer access not only to men of battle such as Hawkwood and Sabraham but also to the source of many of his Italian narratives: the great library at Pavia.

12

The Library at Pavia

Pavia, in the heart of the Po Valley, is still noted for its narrow cobbled lanes, medieval towers, and buildings with terracotta facades. There was certainly ample time for Chaucer to visit Pavia during his 1378 visit to Lombardy. He would have been in Italy for about one and a half months, or the period from approximately 1 July to 15 August.

According to Robert Pratt, the negotiations with John Hawkwood took place in Milan between 15 July and 2 August. 'That would leave two weeks from his arrival in Italy (1 July to 14 July) and thirteen days (3 August to 15 August) after Hawkwood's departure from Milan when Chaucer could have made the easy day's journey to Pavia.' Chaucer had 'ample opportunity – and perhaps a diplomatic duty – to visit Pavia during his second Italian journey'.

Pavia was the domain and power base of Galeazzo II Visconti, who took the town by force in 1359, adding it to the Visconti Milanese territories, soon to become the Duchy of Milan under Galeazzo II's son, Giangaleazzo Visconti. Situated strategically on the River Ticino, Pavia had been an important town in the Roman Empire, when it was known as Ticinum. It later became part of the Lombard Kingdom in the post-Roman period. Chaucer would have been impressed by Pavia's medieval towers, including the eleventh-century 72-metre-high Civic Tower (which sadly collapsed in 1989 and has not been rebuilt); the churches of San Michele Maggiore, San Teodoro, and San Pietro in Ciel d'Oro, where the king of the Lombards, Liutprand, is buried; and above all the Visconti castle or fortress, the Castello Visconteo, built by Galeazzo II as his private residence – and a potent symbol of his power.

Galeazzo II was certainly different from his brother Bernabò. He is still remembered for his invention of a forty-day form of torture called the 'Quaresima', in which prisoners were subjected to ordeals such as the rack, the wheel, eye-gouging, and strappado (being dropped from a height) before being given a day of reprieve – followed by more torture. But the same Galeazzo II was interested in literature and the arts, a patron of Petrarch who sponsored writers and intellectuals and who, under a charter granted by Holy Roman Emperor Charles IV, founded the University of Pavia to teach law, philosophy, medicine, and the liberal arts. He was fashionably stylish, with long golden hair that, we are told, rested on his shoulders in a silken net or was garlanded with flowers. By contrast with Bernabò, who had fourteen legitimate children and twenty-two illegitimate ones by his many mistresses, Galeazzo II had only two offspring, both legitimate: his son (and successor), Giangaleazzo, and his daughter, Violante.

The Pavia library had nearly 1,000 volumes in it, available to visiting scholars, statesmen, and poets. The collection included works by Ovid, Seneca, Virgil, St Augustine, Dante, and even Boccaccio, despite the latter's enmity for the Viscontis. Galeazzo II's imposing Castello Visconteo was partially destroyed by Spanish and French invasions in the sixteenth century, but much of it still survives as a civic museum. The attractions include a huge arcaded courtyard, art and history exhibitions, and the premises (if not the contents) of the former Visconti library, now the frescoed Blue Room, decorated in gold and lapis lazuli.

Then there was Petrarch, who – much to Boccaccio's disgust – had been a celebrity at the Viscontis' courts for fifteen years, on and off, insisting that although he received 'comforts and honours' from them it was to others that they turned for 'advice on the conduct of public affairs'. Pavia would also have had special significance for Chaucer as the place where, in the sixth century, Boethius had written his *Consolation of Philosophy*, on the importance of philosophy for everyday life and times of hardship, before being tortured to death. Chaucer not only translated the work, under the title *Boece*, but he also incorporated many of its ideas into his own work, for example giving a philosophical element to 'The Knight's Tale' that is absent from the original, Boccaccio's *Teseida*.

If it had not been for the Visconti library at Pavia, Chaucer would have been dependent on loans of books from private collections such as that of Petrarch, who is known to have had 200 books and to have employed copyists to reproduce them. Boccaccio's *Teseida* influenced not only Chaucer's 'Knight's Tale' but also his 'Franklin's Tale', *Parliament of Fowls*, and *Legend of Good Women*. The Pavia library may be the answer to the question of where and when Chaucer obtained a copy of the *Teseida*, a matter that has long puzzled scholars, since it has not been found in any medieval English collection, and no contemporary English references to it exist. Robert Pratt has suggested that Chaucer probably obtained the *Teseida* during his 1378 journey to Lombardy, not only because the collections of the Visconti dukes in Milan and Pavia were 'among the greatest in Italy' but also because of the facts that the Viscontis were 'noted for their generosity in allowing copies of their manuscripts to be made, that they had the copyists to do the job, and that they were at the time anxious to ingratiate themselves with their English visitors'.

Originally, both Visconti brothers had fine libraries in their huge palazzi: Bernabò's was in Milan, while Galeazzo II had built his new castle in 1360 at Pavia, 35 km to the south, and had installed a library there when it was completed five years later. But when in 1385 Galeazzo II's son, Giangaleazzo, mounted a coup against Bernabò, imprisoned him, and supposedly caused his death, Bernabò's Milan castle was destroyed, and its contents – including the library – were dispersed. The Pavia library of Galeazzo II, however, survived, and an inventory drawn up in 1426 lists nearly 1,000 books and manuscripts, including two copies of the *Teseida*. Admittedly, this was nearly half a century after Chaucer's visit to Lombardy, but the contents of the Pavia library would almost certainly have been much the same. 'There is no reason why Chaucer might not have visited the Pavia castle in 1378,' William Coleman concludes. 'Chaucer's journey to Bernabò Visconti and John Hawkwood in Milan was, we remember, a diplomatic one: *pro certis negociis expedicionem guerre Regis tangentibus.* Perhaps a courtesy call at the court of the other Lombard duke, Galeazzo II in Pavia, would have been in order.'

Petrarch claimed that Boccaccio's animosity toward the Viscontis prevented him from setting foot in Pavia, but Boccaccio refers to the church of San Pietro in Ciel d'Oro in the *Decameron*, in the tale of Torello (*Decameron* 10:9), a merchant-turned-Crusader from Pavia who is imprisoned in Alexandria but is returned safely to Pavia by Saladin. Chaucer himself refers to Pavia in 'The Merchant's Tale', which is drawn from the *Decameron* and tells the story of a young woman married to a sixty-year-old knight from Pavia – '*Whilom ther was dwelling in Lumbardye a worthy knight, that born was of Pavie*' – who deceives her husband with her lover in a pear tree.

Marion Turner finds it 'overwhelmingly likely' that Chaucer visited the great library of Galeazzo II Visconti at Pavia on the Milan 1378 trip, and that it was there that he read – or even acquired – the Italian works that influenced him. The library inventory includes an extraordinary number of texts also used by Chaucer, many of which were not available in England. Turner notes:

His poetry in the 1380s demonstrates, in particular, extensive knowledge of Boccaccio's poetry at a time when no one else in England seems to have had such knowledge ... Chaucer may well have not only read new texts here but also acquired copies to take back home with him. He got copies of the *Teseida* and the *Filostrato* from somewhere, and this is by far the most likely place.

Chaucer had been inspired in his youth by French poets, but the Italian writers had an equal if not greater effect on him. 'No literary models would influence Chaucer more,' writes Frances Stonor Saunders. 'Dante, Petrarch, and Boccaccio were in his mind, both as their translator and their adapter, for the rest of his life. They changed the direction of his poetry, and therefore the whole development of English literature.'

In Pavia, according to the library inventory, Chaucer would have found Boccaccio's *Filostrato, Amorosa visione, Decameron, De genealogia deorum Gentilium, De mulieribus claris, De casibus virorum illustrium*, and *De Montibus*. The inventory also includes texts by Virgil, Ovid, St Jerome, St Augustine, and Dante, as well as Petrarch, and a large number of French translations of Latin texts by writers such as Boethius. The Castello of Galeazzo II Visconti at Pavia even had a painting of the story of Patient Griselda on the wall of one of its rooms, which Chaucer may well have seen, inspiring him later when he came to write 'The Clerk's Tale'.

The Viscontis, unusually, were known to lend their books and allow others to make copies, and in Pavia there was no lack of scribes – for example, at the scriptorium attached to the church of San Pietro in Ciel d'Oro. One crucial clue is the fact that a copy of Boccaccio's *Teseida* in the inventory has sections missing – and this matches Chaucer's version of the story in 'The Knight's Tale', which omits exactly the same parts, strongly suggesting that Chaucer used a copy he obtained at Pavia.

Courtesy calls and library visits apart, there were further reasons for Chaucer going to Pavia during his time in

Lombardy, one being the death of Galeazzo II Visconti on 4 August 1378 and his burial in the monastery of St Augustine, next to the church of San Pietro in Ciel d'Oro. This would have been a great state event, requiring not only the pomp and circumstance of the Visconti dynasty but the presence of all distinguished visitors – including Chaucer. He would also have been drawn to Pavia because the body of Duke Lionel, who after all was Chaucer's first patron, was interred there, probably in the church of San Pietro, before it was transferred later to Clare in Suffolk for reburial. San Pietro also contains the tombs of both Boethius and St Augustine, and boasts the *ciel d'oro* after which it is named; much of this 'golden sky' has disappeared, but gold-leaf mosaics still decorate the ceiling of the apse.

13

Rome and Avignon

As far as we know, Chaucer did not visit Rome itself during his trips to Italy. The question of loyalty to Rome as the heart of Western Christianity and seat of the papacy did, however, loom very large in his life – and work. As David Benson notes in *Imagined Romes,* the Rome that medieval English travellers experienced was 'radically diminished from its former eminence as the teeming capital of an immense empire': the population had shrunk, and cattle grazed amid the ruins of imperial Rome. Above all, 'medieval Rome had lost its reputation for Christian sanctity': the age of the martyrs was long past, the pope and his court were absent at Avignon for much of the fourteenth century, and the subsequent schism 'further damaged the prestige of the papacy'. As the Welsh priest Adam Usk – a contemporary of Chaucer's – put it, Rome was a place where 'everything was for sale, and benefices were granted not according to merit but to the highest bidder'.

The split in the Church was not resolved in Chaucer's lifetime. By the time he came to write the *Canterbury Tales,* there were two rival popes – Boniface IX in Rome (reigned 1389–1404) and Clement VII in Avignon (reigned 1378–94)

– who excommunicated each other as schismatics and heretics. The Church in England had adapted to the Avignon Papacy after it was first founded in 1309; there was even a chapel at Avignon Cathedral built by an English stonemason called Hugh Wilfrid. Avignon, after all, was a major commercial centre. Iris Origo writes of Avignon in her study of the *Merchant of Prato*:

> It was here that Tuscan merchants came – by sea from
> Pisa to the coast of Provence and then up the Rhone – to
> buy Flemish and English wool and heavy cloth, and to
> sell the fine finished cloth of the *Arte di Calimala* [the
> guild of Florence cloth merchants], the silks and brocades
> of Lucca, the veils of Perugia and Arezzo, the painted
> panels of gold and silverware of Florence.

But England supported the return of the papacy to Rome and the restoration there of Italian pontiffs – first the scrupulous and austere (though notoriously bad-tempered) Urban VI, formerly Bartolomeo Prignano, archbishop of Bari and a Neapolitan by origin, and then his successor, the adroit and outgoing Boniface IX, formerly Pietro Tomacelli, also from Naples. Petrarch wrote that the popes at Avignon had 'strangely forgotten their origin': they were the successors of the 'poor fishermen from Galilee' who had first spread the gospel, but had become rich, were 'loaded with gold and clad in purple', lived in luxurious palaces, and were power-hungry and greedy.

The fact that Chaucer also regretted the split can be inferred from 'The Second Nun's Tale', the story of St Cecilia in Rome, in which he stresses the theme of unity and 'one Christendom'. In this he may well have been inspired by Adam Easton, the Benedictine priest and scholar from Norfolk who was made a cardinal by Pope Urban VI in 1381, who arranged the marriage of Richard II and Anne of Bohemia in Westminster Abbey the following year, and who was given charge as cardinal of the church of Santa Cecilia in Trastevere in Rome, where his magnificent tomb can still be admired.

In his Tales, Chaucer accuses friars of lechery, gluttony, avarice, and pride – the very sins his mentor Petrarch attributed to the cardinals of the Avignon Curia, repeatedly describing Avignon in his *Canzoniere* poems as 'Babylon', a place of exile. The schism was seen by many as a sign of divine punishment for 'the sins and pride of the clergy', not least by Vincent Ferrer of Valencia, known as the 'Angel of the Apocalypse', who became an itinerant preacher in Europe for twenty years, predicting the end of the world.

Criticism of corruption and venality within the Church predated the schism. But the schism did highlight what was widely seen as moral disorder brought about by the sins of those running the Church. Chaucer implicitly contrasts the virtues of the early Church in the story of Cecilia with the greed and corruption of the modern Church as represented by the corrupt Summoner and Pardoner, the avaricious Friar, the lukewarm Prioress, and the pampered Monk. The Monk is a 'fat and personable priest' who wears 'fine grey fur, the finest in the land', and who, far from being 'pale like a tormented soul', has the complexion of one who enjoys his food – 'he liked a fat swan best, and roasted whole'. The Monk's main interest is hunting, and the bridle on his horse rings 'as loud as does the chapel bell where my lord Monk was prior of the cell'.

The Monk is asked to tell his story as the pilgrims are approaching the cathedral city of Rochester, with Harry Bailly remarking on his girth – 'You're nothing like a ghost or penitent!' – and observing that if he were pope he would make sure all clerics had wives to keep them in order and give them children. Then there is Hubert, the 'wanton' and 'merry' Friar, who had arranged many a marriage for 'his young women' and had a special licence from the pope to hear confession from 'city dames of honour and possessions' – 'or so he said'. He kept trinkets 'to give to pretty girls', loved singing and 'played the hurdy-gurdy', and 'knew the taverns well in every town, and every innkeeper and barmaid too'. Friar Hubert, we are told, thought it beneath his dignity to deal with lepers or 'slum-and-gutter dwellers', preferring the company of the rich 'anywhere a profit might accrue'. He expected 'a gift' for giving a penitent sinner absolution, was adept at extracting a farthing from a poor widow, and avoided a 'threadbare habit', preferring to dress 'more like a doctor or a pope', his clothes 'swelling … like a bell' because of his rotund figure.

The Summoner, so called because he summoned sinners to ecclesiastical trials, was 'hot and lecherous as a sparrow', given to imbibing 'strong red wine till all was hazy', and 'shout[ing] and jabber[ing] as if crazy' so that 'children were afraid when he appeared', but beneath it all calculating whom he could threaten with excommunication – 'he knew their secrets, they did what he said' – and extracting bribes from those who hoped to avoid it: 'why, he'd allow – just for a quart of wine – any good lad to keep a concubine a twelvemonth'.

The Summoner is furious when the Friar tells the story of another summoner who is dragged to Hell 'body and soul' by the Devil after trying to extract a bribe from a poor widow on the basis of false accusations of sin. He retorts that it is no wonder the Friar knows about devils, since 'friars and fiends are seldom far asunder'. He then retaliates with the bawdy tale of a friar in Yorkshire who cadges food and drink from everyone and takes money to say 'trentals' (thirty masses) for the souls of those in Purgatory, but who is fooled by a man ill in bed who promises the friar a secret gift if he puts his hand on his backside, then lets out a resounding fart.

As for the Pardoner, authorised to sell pardons and indulgences – remissions of punishment in Purgatory after death for sins committed in life – he has 'a holy relic on his cap' and a wallet 'brimful of pardons come from Rome'. He also has any number of fake relics – the Virgin Mary's veil, part of the sail from St Peter's boat when Christ walked on the water, a collection of saints' – or rather pigs' – bones with which to fool country parsons – and 'by his flatteries and prevarication made monkeys of the priest and congregation'.

'The Pardoner's Tale' is clearly linked to *Decameron* 6:10, the story of Friar Cipolla of the Order of St Anthony in the Val d'Elsa near Florence, a 'cheerful rascal' who keeps what he claims is a feather of the angel Gabriel in a casket. When some local tricksters put coals in the casket instead, the Friar claims they are the coals on which St Lawrence was burned to death, thus continuing to gather offerings 'to his considerable profit'.

Both the Pardoner and Friar Cipolla are corrupt preachers who exploit credulous people by using (or misusing) fake relics.

But then there is the Parson, a 'holy minded man of good renown ... who truly knew Christ's gospel and would preach it devoutly to parishioners, and teach it', calling on all his flock, however remote, and giving to the poor not only from church offerings but also from his own pocket rather than 'singing masses for the wealthy dead'. Chaucer concludes, 'I think there never was a better priest.' Asked to tell the final story as the pilgrims approach Canterbury, the Parson reminds them that St Paul in his Epistle to Timothy 'reproves all those who waive aside the truth for fables that are wretched and uncouth', and he gives them a sermon on penitence and the seven deadly sins.

Above all, there is the Prioress, Madame Eglantine – dainty, elegant, and neat, 'dignified in all her dealings' and distressed if she so much as sees a mouse caught in a trap – and her secretary, the Second Nun, who tells the story of St Cecilia. The Prioress, we are told, is from Stratford: not Stratford-upon-Avon but the Benedictine nunnery or priory of St Leonard's at Stratford-at-Bow in East London, of which only part of the churchyard remains. The Prioress is not exactly ideal: as Eileen Power notes in *Medieval People*, she is clearly from a rather 'snobbish convent', well bred, with beautiful table manners, wears a gold brooch, likes 'pretty clothes and little dogs', and has a straight nose, grey eyes, and a little red mouth, a description 'which might have been taken straight out of one of the feudal books of deportment for girls'. Her manner is rather precious, and the story she tells is decidedly anti-Semitic, blaming the Jews in an unnamed Asian town for murdering a Christian boy for singing a hymn to the Virgin Mary, *O Alma Redemptoris Mater*.

Rather more straightforward is the Second Nun, who relates the story of the Roman virgin martyr St Cecilia, the 'Lily of Heaven' and the patron saint of musicians. Cecilia, we are told, was married but wore a hair shirt on her wedding night and told her husband, Valerian, that an angel would kill him if he so much as touched her. Instead of protesting, Valerian converted to Christianity and went to heaven when the local Roman governor had him killed. The story stresses Cecilia's chastity and her endurance in the face of torture and death despite facing the might of the Roman Empire. Chaucer's life of St Cecilia is a translation – sometimes word for word – of the *Golden Legend* by the thirteenth-century archbishop of Genoa, Jacobus de Varagine, who was born Jacopo de Fazio at Varagine (now Varazze), on the Ligurian coast, between Genoa and Savona.

Then, just as the pilgrims reach the village of Boughton under Blean, 8 km from Canterbury, two latecomers appear: a Canon, dressed in black, and his servant or Yeoman. Chaucer here reverts to criticism of religious hypocrisy: the Yeoman reveals that a certain canon – evidently his own priestly boss, a man of 'endless tricks and cunning' – is guilty of having tricked a fellow priest into believing he has turned base metal into silver through alchemy and the search for the mythical Philosopher's Stone. One theory is that Chaucer had himself been fooled by an alchemist. The Yeoman stresses that not all priests are crooks and asks the 'holy canons of the church' to remember that among the twelve Apostles there was only one traitor, namely Judas. 'God knows, there is some sneaking rascal in every house', but 'if any lurking Judas should appear among you, fling him out I say betimes, before you're shamed and beggared by his crimes'.

There was an emerging protest movement in the church at the time: the Lollards, a derogatory term derived from the Dutch term for 'mumblers'. The Lollards were followers of John Wycliffe, an Oxford theologian who in many ways anticipated the Protestant Reformation by demanding that the scriptures be available in English rather than Latin; condemning prayers to saints, the worship of images, and enforced clerical celibacy; and dismissing transubstantiation, the Catholic belief that the bread and wine at Communion not only represent the body and blood of Christ but become them, as a 'feigned miracle'.

Chaucer may have known Wycliffe personally, since both had John of Gaunt as their patron and protector. Wycliffe was not immediately seen as a heretic: after all, anticlerical criticism (such as Chaucer's) was not uncommon. Chaucer would have been aware that Cardinal Easton, the most powerful Englishman in the papal Curia, clearly shared Wycliffe's dislike of wealthy and corrupt friars. In the end, however, the Church authorities – including Easton – came to defend the institution against increasingly withering attacks by Wycliffe, with the English cardinal issuing a weighty justification of papal authority entitled *Defence of Ecclesiastical Power*.

Wycliffe's Bible came to be condemned not just because it was in English but also because it did not have the obligatory commentary, or 'gloss', to ensure the text was not 'misinter-preted'. Wycliffe welcomed the schism between Rome and Avignon as a prelude to the destruction of the papacy, which he regarded as a misused power base with no scriptural valid-ity. As a result, Lollards came to be seen as heretics, and although Wycliffe himself escaped trial and died a natural death in 1384, many Lollards were persecuted and put to death in the fifteenth century.

Dante Gabriel Rossetti is later said to have believed – absurdly – that Chaucer went to Italy to escape the wrath of the clergy in England and to seek the protection of Petrarch and Boccaccio, who were supposedly part of a secret society to destroy the corrupt papacy. More plausibly, John Foxe in his *Actes and Monuments* – better known as the Book of Martyrs, a seminal founding work of Protestantism, first published in English in 1563 – hails Chaucer as a '*right Wiclevian*' because of his anticlerical caricatures. Chaucer was connected to a number of well-placed men in the royal household who found Wycliffe's religious arguments persuasive and became known as the 'Lollard Knights', such as Thomas Latimer, William Neville, William Beauchamp, and Lewis Clifford, all of whom – like Chaucer himself – were close to John of Gaunt.

For Nicholas Watson, 'there is nothing inherently false about sixteenth-century Protestant attempts to claim Chaucer as at least a moderate Wycliffite precursor'. Chaucer 'may or may not have been interested in all the ideas associated with Lollardy', but his pilgrims on their way to buy indulgences at the Canterbury shrine of St Thomas Becket certainly 'begin to look uncomfortably like a group of false hypocrites'. As such, the *Canterbury Tales* 'can be understood both as an optimistic account of a Christian community journeying towards salvation and as a pessimistic attack on a society whose members mostly merit damnation'.

On the other hand, Chaucer's direct references to the Lollards in the *Canterbury Tales* are not exactly complimentary. After 'The Man of Law's Tale', the story of a Syrian sultan who converts from Islam to Christianity for love of the Roman emperor's daughter, Harry Bailly turns to the Parson and asks him to tell the next tale, exclaiming, 'God's bones, Sir Parish Priest, tell us a tale! ... You learned men are full of ancient lore. God's dignity!' The Parson, however, is offended by the references to God, saying '*Benedictie*!' ('bless us all!'), and adding, 'What ails the man so sinfully to swear?'

'I smell a Lollard in the wind,' says Bailly, an apparent reference to the Parson's Puritanism. He warns the pilgrims they are in for a sermon (a 'predication'), for 'this Lollard here would like to preach, that's what'. The Shipman then steps in and offers to tell his story instead, so that the Parson will not 'vex us with this preaching, his commentaries and his gospel-teaching. We all believe in God round here ... and he'll go starting up some heresy and sow his tares in our clean corn', a reference to the parable of the good and bad seeds in Matthew 13:24–43.

For G. K. Chesterton, author of the Father Brown stories and a prominent convert from Anglicanism to Roman Catholicism, Chaucer was 'clothed in scarlet' and 'emblazoned with the Sacred Heart'. Linda Georgianna argues that much study of Chaucer and religion has been dominated by a 'Protestant bias' that misrepresents and misunderstands Chaucer's Catholic beliefs. From the Reformation onward, there was a 'near unanimity of opinion' that Chaucer had been 'a proto-Protestant, anticlerical poet', Georgianna suggests. But that reputation is based not only on Chaucer's stories but also on the mistaken attribution to him of the spurious 'Plowman's Tale', 'a Lollard attack on clerical power'.

Many of the brothels in Southwark, the area of London from which Chaucer's Canterbury pilgrims set out, were owned or licensed by the Church, and the Tabard Inn itself was owned by the abbot of the Benedictine Abbey of Hyde at Winchester. But Chaucer's attitudes toward the malpractices of the Church should not be confused with his attitudes toward Christianity. Like the Lollards, Chaucer regarded many in the Roman Catholic Church hierarchy as venal and corrupt, but he remained loyal, as his extraordinary retraction at the end of the *Canterbury Tales* clearly shows.

In the retraction, Chaucer begs 'all those that listen to this little treatise, or read it if there be anything in it that pleases them, they thank Our Lord Jesu Christ for it, from whom proceeds all understanding and goodness'. In this, as in so much else, Chaucer was following the example of Boccaccio, who in the *Decameron* was equally scathing about lustful and corrupt friars and clerics but in an afterword defends himself for telling such scurrilous tales. Although he has told the truth about friars, Boccaccio says, they are on the whole 'good people' (even if they stink a bit) who 'flee the world's discomforts for the love of God'. 'What books, what words, what letters are holier, worthier, more venerable than those of the Divine Scriptures? ... I humbly thank Him, who after so long a labour has brought us with His help to the desired conclusion'.

Chaucer is even more repentant in his own afterword to the *Canterbury Tales*. He had earlier been asked by Harry Bailly to tell a story himself, but his 'Tale of Sir Topas' is eventually interrupted by Bailly, who dismisses it as dreary and illiterate doggerel – a marvellous piece of drollery on Chaucer's part, given that he has of course written all the other stories himself.

Instead of 'Sir Topas', he tells the story of Melibee, who, on the insistence of his wife, Dame Prudence, forgives burglars who have injured his daughter, Sophia – and, once again, the story comes from an Italian source: Albertanus of Brescia's twelfth-century *Liber consolationis et consilii*. Melibee forgives in a spirit of Christian mercy derived from the gospels, which, as Chaucer explains, were written by four different Evangelists because 'no one Evangelist would have sufficed to tell us of the pains of Jesus Christ'.

This devotion to the Bible is reinforced in the retraction at the end of the book. The section is headed '*Heere taketh the makere of this book his leve*', and some see the retraction as little more than a conventional epilogue, not uncommon in the European literature of the time. It is also pointed out that the narrator of the *Canterbury Tales* is not necessarily the same as Chaucer himself but is another of his inventions: he was, in effect, one of his own characters. But the retraction is clearly Chaucer himself speaking – and Chaucer asks the reader 'meekly for the mercy of God to pray for me, that Christ have mercy on me and forgive me my sins'. He especially revokes any passages that promote 'worldly vanities', not only in the *Canterbury Tales* but also in *Troilus and Criseyde*, the *House of Fame*, the *Parliament of Fowls*, the *Book of the Duchess* and 'many a song and many a lecherous lay ... [may] Christ in his great mercy forgive me the sin'.

By contrast, Chaucer thanks Jesus, 'His blissful Mother', and 'all the Saints of Heaven' for his translation of Boethius' *Consolation of Philosophy*, and 'other books of Saints' legends, of homilies, and morality and devotion'. He hopes they will send him the grace 'to bewail my sins and to study the salvation of my soul' through penitence and confession, 'so that I may be one of those that at the Day of Judgement shall be saved'. And so, 'here ends the book of the *Tales of Canterbury* compiled by Geoffrey Chaucer, on whose soul Jesu Christ have mercy'.

As Derek Pearsall has observed, in referring to Lollardy, Chaucer is 'his usual cautious and evasive self'. In his 1891 *Studies in Chaucer*, the Yale professor Thomas Lounsbury concluded that Chaucer was not a Lollard: his business was 'the portrayal of men as they are, and not the effort to make them what they ought to be, or what he thought they ought to be.' Chaucer was witheringly critical of the clerical sins that the Rome–Avignon rivalry had highlighted. But, in the end, he sought to improve the Church rather than revolutionise it.

14

The Later Years

Chaucer never returned to Italy after his 1378 mission – but Italy, like France, continued to enrich his output as he became a celebrated author. Chaucer likely wrote his 'dream vision', the *House of Fame,* just after his return from Lombardy; the *Parliament of Fowls* – a celebration of St Valentine's Day and the coming of spring, in which three male eagles compete for the love of a female eagle (in vain; she postpones her decision for a year) – some two years later; the *Legend of Good Women,* which retells, among others, the stories of Antony and Cleopatra, Pyramus and Thisbe, and Dido and Aeneas, in about 1386; and *Troilus and Crysede* at about the same time.

All of these draw on the 'classical style' of both Dante and Boccaccio: Chaucer's source for the tale of Antony and Cleopatra, for example, was Boccaccio's *De casibus virorum illustrium* and *De mulieribus claris,* which also inspired the story of Zenobia in 'The Monk's Tale'. Chaucer also found time to translate the *Consolation of Philosophy* by Boethius (or Boece, as Chaucer calls him), the Roman philosopher who, as we have seen, was put to death in Pavia in the sixth century, and to write his *Treatise on the Astrolabe* for his ten-year-old son Lewis. The treatise was one of the first examples of technical and scientific writing in the English language, the astrolabe being an instrument used not only for horoscopes (frequently mentioned in Chaucer's tales, not least by the Wife of Bath) but also to calculate the position of the sun and stars.

Chaucer held the job of comptroller of customs for twelve years, from 1374 until 1386, while also writing some of his most famous and popular works. These were circulated in written form as well as read aloud, with Chaucer himself apparently performing to Richard II and members of the royal household, at least according to an illustration in one surviving manuscript of *Troilus and Criseyde* (though Richard's features were later erased after Henry IV came to power). Chaucer continued to collect the 'gallon of wine daily' granted to him by Edward III in 1374 for 'the rest of his life' – until Richard II became king three years later, after which this privilege was converted into a more-than-adequate annual pension of 20 pounds (roughly 25,000 pounds per year in today's money).

There was one troubling personal episode in Chaucer's later life. In 1380 – just two years after the trip to Lombardy – one Cecily Chaumpaigne (or Champaigne) accused him of *raptus* (rape), and Chaucer settled with her out of court. Haldeen Braddy notes the coincidence that Chaucer lost his post as comptroller of customs and his Aldgate lease – supposedly also granted to him for life – not long after the downfall of Alice Perrers, mistress of Edward III, and has suggested – though some Chaucer scholars have dismissed this – that Cecily Chaumpaigne was Alice's daughter or stepdaughter. Braddy has even speculated that Chaucer's son Lewis may have been the result of his encounter with Cecily Chaumpaigne.

Other scholars have put forward arguments for Chaucer's innocence. '*Raptus*' can mean abduction rather than rape, and Chaucer was fully exonerated by Cecily Chaumpaigne – once he had paid her compensation. There was no reference to violation or deflowering in the charge, as would have usually been the case. In a memorandum issued three days after the first 'release', Cecily, instead of repeating the charge of *raptus,* exonerated Chaucer in much more general terms, releasing him from 'all manner of actions' concerning 'felonies, trespasses, accounts, debts, and any other actions whatsoever'. Christopher Cannon of Johns Hopkins University, who discovered this second document in the Public Records Office, notes that all mentions of rape had been 'quietly, but emphatically, retracted'. Sebastian Sobecki, meanwhile, has suggested that Chaucer was the guardian of a young man called Edmund Staplegate, the son of a Canterbury merchant, and that if Cecily was 'abducted' by Chaucer it would have been in order to acquire a possible wife for his ward.

Whatever the truth, the incident seems to have been resolved quickly with an exchange of money, possibly through an intermediary, in June 1380. No doubt Chaucer was helped by the fact that a number of powerful men testified as to his good character, including William Beauchamp, chamberlain of the king's household, and William Neville, admiral of the fleet.

The other major event for Chaucer after his return from Lombardy was the Peasants' Revolt in 1381, largely prompted by protests against taxation to raise money for the war with

France. The revolt was led by Wat Tyler, who marched with Kentish rebels from Canterbury to London – the reverse of the route taken by Chaucer's pilgrims – and negotiated a peace with Richard II himself at Smithfield, only to be betrayed by the king and stabbed to death in the melee that followed the confrontation.

The uprising, which began as a protest against repeated poll taxes, developed into a wider revolt against serfdom, epitomised by a rhyme popularised by the radical clergyman John Ball: 'When Adam delved and Eve span, who was then the gentleman?' The rebels demanded that 'henceforward no man should be a serf', and that peasants should hold land 'at their own will forever, freely, and not at the will of the lord'. They failed, but serfdom was all but abolished within a hundred years.

One of the many victims of the uprising was Simon Sudbury, the archbishop of Canterbury and lord chancellor, who had crowned Richard II in July 1377. His body was buried at Canterbury Cathedral, but his head, which had been impaled by the rebels on London Bridge, was – and still is – preserved at the church of St Gregory Sudbury in Suffolk, his birthplace. When the uprising was suppressed, John Ball was hung, drawn, and quartered at St Albans, and his head was also stuck on a pike at London Bridge.

It is not known if Chaucer was in the City of London at the time of the Peasants' Revolt, but if he was he would have seen its leaders pass almost directly under his window at Aldgate. Perhaps he was in hiding: Chaucer would have been a natural target for the rebels, given his government positions and his close association with John of Gaunt, whose Savoy Palace (later the site of a prison, a hospital, and ultimately the present Savoy Hotel) was burned to the ground in the uprising, with the rebels hurling jewels, silk hangings, and gold and silver vessels into the Thames. In a 'bacchanalian orgy', as Helen Carr puts it in her biography of John, they drank his wine in the cellars and mistakenly rolled barrels of gunpowder into the fire, causing an explosion that demolished what was left of the palace.

Flemish weavers were a particular target of the rebels' wrath, and there was an infamous massacre of Flemings who had taken refuge in St Martin Vintry, Chaucer's own boyhood church, close to his lodgings at Aldgate. Their bodies were dumped in the Thames. However, Chaucer makes no reference to the revolt in his works, apart from one mention of a farmyard riot in 'The Nun's Priest's Tale', which talks of the dogs, ducks, and geese making a '*hydous ... noyse*' such as even Jack Straw and his men '*ne made nevere shoutes half so shrille whan that they wolden any Flemyng kille*'. Possibly this reticence is due to the fact that Chaucer was in the service of Richard II himself – who was still only fourteen at the time of the rebellion – and to comment on the uprising or the death of Wat Tyler would have been unwise. Like Tyler, Chaucer had a Kent connection: while still working as comptroller, he was appointed as a 'commissioner of peace' for Kent in the 1380s, at a time when French invasion was a possibility.

It was in the Kent period that Chaucer started work on the *Canterbury Tales*, which would have taken his mind back to Italy and the tales of Petrarch and Boccaccio: he had already written several of the *Canterbury Tales*, including 'The Knight's Tale' and 'The Second Nun's Tale' of the life of St Cecilia, but now he started composing the pilgrims' tales in the form of a journey to Canterbury. He never quite completed it; the manuscript was left unfinished and was put together in book form after his death, probably by his copyist, or scrivener, Adam Pinkhurst. Chaucer wrote a poem of mild complaint to Pinkhurst ('*so ofte aday I mot thy werk renewe, it to correcte and eke to rubbe and scrape*') from which we know that Adam also produced manuscript copies of *Boece* and *Troilus and Criseyde*. As the Tales became popular, other scribes later copied them too, though some added their own amendments, with one noting at the end of 'The Knight's Tale', '*Iste fabula est valde absurda*' ('this story is completely absurd').

Canterbury was chosen not just because of Chaucer's Kent connections but also because of the tomb of St Thomas Becket, which had become an instant shrine once pilgrims gained access to it in April 1171, with many miracles of healing attributed to it. Just two years later, in 1173, Becket was made a saint, and the following year Henry II performed an act of penance at the shrine for having – whether knowingly or not – caused Becket's murder by asking 'Will no one rid me of this turbulent priest?' There was a fire shortly after this act of remorse, and in 1220 a magnificent new tomb was unveiled. It remained an object of veneration in Chaucer's time and for well over a hundred years after that, until it was destroyed on the orders of Henry VIII in 1538.

In addition to compiling the Tales, Chaucer became a member of Parliament for Kent in 1386, and attended the

'Wonderful Parliament' that year, so called because it sought to counteract the increasingly despotic reign of Richard II and dismissed his lord chancellor, Michael de la Pole, for the corrupt use of public funds that Parliament assigned instead to sea and land defences. Chaucer appears to have been present on most of the seventy-one days Parliament sat, for which he was paid 24 pounds and 9 shillings. On 15 October that year, he gave his deposition in the case of Scrope versus Grosvenor, which, as we have seen, gives us a clue to his date of birth.

There is no further reference after this date to Philippa, Chaucer's wife, and she is presumed to have died in 1387. It seems they had, in any case, drifted apart. At the end of 1386, Chaucer lost his job as comptroller of customs, possibly because John of Gaunt, his patron, was absent on a military expedition to Spain. This was a politically difficult, even dangerous, period: a group of senior aristocrats known as the Lords Appellant, including Edward III's son Thomas of Woodstock and his grandson Henry Bolingbroke (the son of John of Gaunt, and the future Henry IV), impeached and executed some of Richard II's advisers at the so-called Merciless Parliament of 1388.

The Lords Appellant were, for the most part, disenchanted not only with the failures of the Hundred Years' War with France – there had been few victories to celebrate – but also with its exorbitant cost, paid for by taxation. Blaming Richard's court for corruption and failure of leadership, they in effect mounted a coup against the monarch, defeating his forces at the Battle of Radcot Bridge (a medieval structure that still spans the Thames near Oxford) and reducing the king to a figurehead. Richard regained power, however, and several of the rebellious Lords Appellant were executed during the 1390s, including Thomas of Woodstock (duke of Gloucester) and Richard Fitzalan (earl of Arundel), while Thomas de Beauchamp (earl of Warwick) was exiled for life to the Isle of Man.

Chaucer, as usual, kept his head down. Possibly he shared their disillusionment with the war, which, after all, he had himself experienced at first hand as a young man: his poem 'The Former Age' and above all his 'Tale of Melibee' in the *Canterbury Tales* appear to favour the peaceful settlement of issues rather than meeting violence with violence. He seems to have retreated from public life at this point – understandably – until the return of John of Gaunt from Spain in 1389 enabled Richard II – John of Gaunt's nephew – to resume power. The two men had their differences, but Richard, now in his early twenties, was reconciled with his uncle and adopted Lancastrian rather than Plantagenet emblems.

Chaucer's career as a royal adviser then also resumed: on 12 July 1389, he was appointed clerk of the King's Works, an important post in which he oversaw repairs on Westminster Palace and St George's Chapel at Windsor, and continued building the wharf at the Tower of London. The job paid 2 shillings a day, more than three times his salary as comptroller, and put him in close contact with the king's celebrated master mason, Henry Yeveley, the most important builder of the Middle Ages, who designed Westminster Hall, the tomb of the Black Prince, and the naves of both Westminster Abbey and Canterbury Cathedral. There may even be a link to 'The Knight's Tale', since Chaucer's duties included the construction of stands for spectators watching the jousting tournaments at Smithfields. Chaucer was also appointed keeper of the lodge at the king's park in the royal Feckenham Forest, in Worcestershire, though the records suggest Chaucer's duties as a paymaster made him a target for highway thieves: he was robbed at least three times in 1390, and possibly injured. He stopped working at Feckenham on 17 June 1391. He then became deputy forester in another royal forest, North Petherton Park, in Somerset, on 22 June in that year, though that was possibly something of a sinecure.

But then came a change of regime: in 1399, Richard II was deposed by Henry Bolingbroke, who, as grandson of Edward III, was Richard's cousin. Bolingbroke had been banished by Richard, but he returned from exile and defeated Richard's forces, becoming Henry IV. Richard is said to have been starved to death in February 1400 while held captive at Pontefract in Yorkshire. Chaucer survived the regime change; he seems to have been respected by Henry IV and perhaps even admired. As Henry of Derby, the future king had even given Chaucer fur with which to make a fine coat.

Chaucer, in other words, certainly did not fall out of favour as he approached his end: after all, he was a close friend and brother-in-law of Henry's father, John of Gaunt, the wealthy duke of Lancaster. Chaucer was given a fifty-three-year lease on a residence next to the Lady Chapel within the close of the then-Benedictine abbey at Westminster on 24 December 1399, at a rent of 53 shillings and 4 pence a year, as well as a 'scarlet robe trimmed with fur'. Chaucer even appears to have made one last diplomatic mission, to Calais, early in 1400, shortly before he died. The last mention of Chaucer in the records is on 5 June 1400, when some money was paid that was owed to him. Chaucer died of unknown causes on 25 October 1400, although the only evidence for this date comes from the engraving on his tomb, which was erected more than one hundred years after his death.

Chaucer was buried in Westminster Abbey, as was his right, owing to his status as a tenant of the abbey's close. In 1556, his remains were transferred to a more ornate tomb in the south transept, making him the first writer interred in the area now known as Poets' Corner. The inscription is in Latin; the abbey's translation reads, 'Of old the bard who struck the noblest strains, great Geoffrey Chaucer now this tomb retains'.

Conclusion

Chaucer the *Poeta Elegante*

Chaucer is still widely read, nearly 700 years after his birth. For Paul Strohm, only Chaucer (or perhaps Shakespeare) 'could have dreamed up a group as socially diverse as Chaucer's pilgrims', ranging from the virtuous Knight and the austerely devout Parson to the hypocritical and genteel Prioress, and 'outright scoundrels' such as the false-relic-selling Pardoner, the foul-mouthed Miller, and the garlic-chomping Summoner.

What Chaucer could hardly have guessed at, Strohm adds, is 'the affinity that readers today would feel with this wildly mixed band of tale-tellers; their stylistically varied stories seem tailor-made for the twenty-first century'. For David Wallace, Chaucer is now 'a medieval poet enjoying a global renaissance', with poets, translators, and audiences all over the world finding him an inspiration, from Iran to Japan.

Yet although Chaucer's works had long been admired, serious scholarly work on his legacy did not begin until the late eighteenth century, when Thomas Tyrwhitt edited a new edition of the *Canterbury Tales*, and his oeuvre did not become an established academic discipline until the

nineteenth century. Frederick James Furnivall founded the
Chaucer Society in 1868 and pioneered editions of Chaucer's major texts, along with analyses of Chaucer's language.
Walter William Skeat established the texts of all of Chaucer's works with his edition of *The Complete Works of Geoffrey
Chaucer*, published by Oxford Clarendon Press in 1894–7.
Later editions by John H. Fisher and Larry D. Benson offered
further refinements, along with critical commentary and bib-
liographies. *The Chaucer Review* was founded in 1966 and
has maintained its position as the pre-eminent journal of
Chaucer studies.

It is only recently, by contrast, that Chaucer has been celebrated in the country from which he drew so much of his
material: Italy. As Caron Cioffi noted in 'The First Italian Essay
on Chaucer' in *The Chaucer Review* in 1987, 'The country that
gave so much poetic inspiration and material to Chaucer
was very late in recognising how well those literary loans had
been used.' Chaucer was 'practically unknown' in Italy until
the nineteenth century, though there was a pen portrait of
'Galfredo Chaucero' in Gerolamo Ghilini's *Teatro d'huomini
letterati* of 1647, which claims (wrongly) that Chaucer was an
'illustrious knight and son of a knight' who was born in '*Vuod-
stoc, vicino ad Oxenford*' ('Woodstock, near Oxford'). Ghilini
correctly records, on the other hand, that Chaucer became an
'elegant poet' who imitated Dante and Petrarch 'and others',
and who passed on at a ripe old age. Ghilini, who studied law
in Padua but became a priest at the church of St Ambrose in
Milan, almost certainly drew on *Relationem historicarum de
rebus anglicis* by John Pits, published in Paris in 1619, which

in turn copied the (often erroneous) details of Chaucer's biography in the *Scriptorum illustrium maioris Brytanniae* ('lives of English writers') compiled by the sixteenth-century bishop John Bale.

As George E. Dorris noted in 'The First Italian Criticism of Chaucer and Shakespeare' in 1965, considering Chaucer's debt to Italy, 'it is surprising how little interest Italy had taken in Chaucer until recently'. The first published mention of Chaucer in Italian was by Paolo Rolli in 1730 – but Rolli lived in England. Shakespeare, Milton, and Pope were translated into Italian in the eighteenth-century period of Anglomania in Europe, but Chaucer was not. But then, in 1958, Mario Praz, who had taught Italian at the University of Manchester and English at the University of Rome, devoted his study *The Flaming Heart* to English literature 'from Chaucer to T. S. Eliot', concluding that Chaucer had been greatly influenced by Petrarch and Boccaccio, though he found Chaucer's sense of humour cruder, even in some places 'grotesque'.

Fourteen years later came Pier Paolo Pasolini's groundbreaking 1972 film *I racconti di Canterbury*, first seen at the Berlin Film Festival, with the director himself playing Chaucer, seen at the start jotting down what the pilgrims say as they gather at the Tabard Inn before setting off. The film, which revels in the bawdy debauchery of some of the Tales and was scandalous at the time for its nudity and violence, retells eight of the stories: 'The Merchant's Tale', 'The Friar's Tale', 'The Cook's Tale', 'The Miller's Tale', 'The Wife of Bath's Prologue', 'The Reeve's Tale', 'The Pardoner's Tale', and 'The Summoner's Tale'. Unlike Chaucer's original, in which Canterbury is never reached, the film shows the pilgrims – played by a mix of British and Italian actors – arriving at Canterbury Cathedral and ends with Chaucer (Pasolini) starting to compose their tales at home. Tellingly, he is also seen chuckling over the *Decameron*, and only starts to write his own versions when scolded by his wife. The film was shot in England and recorded in English, with the dialogue later dubbed into Italian. Most of the music is anachronistic, consisting of much later English folk songs, apart from *Veni Sancte Spiritus* ('come Holy Spirit'), a sequence from the medieval Mass for Pentecost.

Pasolini's film coincided with – and possibly reinforced – renewed Italian interest in Chaucer and the publication of Italian versions of the *Canterbury Tales*, such as the translations by Ermanno Barisone (published by Mondadori), professor of English at Genoa University, and by Cesare Foligno (published by Rizzoli), former Serena professor of Italian at Oxford, edited and with an introduction by Attilio Brilli, professor of Anglo-American Studies at the University of Siena. Foligno and Brilli drew on an 1897 translation by Cino Chiarini, an Anglophile professor at the Liceo Classico in Pesaro, whose version of selected Tales was published by Sansoni in Florence, and who met and corresponded with Frederick Furnivall, the founder of the Chaucer Society.

The image that persists, though, is that of Pasolini as Chaucer, a medieval arming cap over his head, absorbed in Boccaccio's *Decameron* and enjoying it hugely before writing down his own stories. Chaucer's visits to Italy were diplomatic missions, involving politics, finance, and trade. But they had a much more lasting effect because of the huge impact on Chaucer of Italian culture and language, which he first got to know when growing up on the banks of the Thames in London, and which he later absorbed to an even greater extent when working as a customs agent in the same district, a few steps from his childhood home.

As a government official, Chaucer spent time in Milan, Genoa, and Florence, and probably in Pavia, Arqua, and Certaldo too, conversing with Italian public figures, traders, bankers – and writers. The impact of *Ytaille* on a man who – whether he knew it or not – was laying the foundations of writing in English was profound and long-lasting. It is perhaps not going too far to say that, thanks to the *Canzoniere* and the *Decameron*, Petrarch and Boccaccio are as much the fathers of English literature as Chaucer himself.

Acknowledgements

Geoffrey Chaucer's life is better documented than the lives of many figures in the Middle Ages. But there are still numerous gaps and uncertainties that have kept Chaucer scholars busy for decades speculating exactly where he went, who he saw, and what he did. As James Root Hulbert of the University of Chicago put it rather waspishly in 1912 in *Chaucer's Official Life*, 'Writers on Chaucer's life have not been content merely to state the facts revealed in the records, but in their eagerness to get closer to Chaucer have drawn many questionable inferences from those facts.'

Or, as the Oxford medieval historian Laura Ashe suggested in *History Today* in 2019, 'It isn't really possible to write a biography of Chaucer', because the documents about his life form such a patchy and at times perplexing picture. The foremost medieval English poet, Ashe comments, is found in the historical records as the recipient of payments and annuities from the king, as a controller of customs, as a soldier and international traveller and emissary, even as a man who avoided a charge of 'rape' by paying damages to the plaintiff, but there is comparatively little about his life as a writer.

There is none the less a great deal of evidence for reconstructing the travels of Chaucer – above all, to Italy. As

Warren Ginsberg has noted, 'Chaucer was the only poet of his day who visited Italy and created poems that were based on works by its most renowned authors.' What I have tried to do is follow in Chaucer's footsteps – to Milan, Genoa, Florence, Pavia, and beyond – and describe what he would have seen and experienced.

The 1966 *Chaucer Life-Records*, drawn from records in the National Archives and edited by Martin Crow and Clair Olson, are an invaluable resource, as are the records of the *Foedera*, or Crown treaties with foreign powers, published by Thomas Rymer and reproduced in 1869 by Thomas Duffus Hardy, and the *Calendar of the Patent Rolls Preserved in the Public Record Office*, held by the University of California and available online from the HathiTrust Digital Library. Documents relating to Chaucer's life are also reproduced on *Harvard's Geoffrey Chaucer Website*. Between them, these sources provide details of Chaucer's public life as a court official, diplomat, and wool-trade controller. But they reveal little about his life as a writer (or 'maker', as writers like Chaucer tended to be called): I have here offered my own interpretation of Chaucer's travels, focusing on his trips to Italy and his involvement with Italian culture and literature, arguing that he not only knew the works of Petrarch and Boccaccio but also drew on them extensively.

This is not to say that Chaucer simply copied the Italian originals, rather that he borrowed from them when it suited him and used his genius to transform their stories into something quintessentially English. In *A Companion to Chaucer*, David Wallace suggests that Chaucer was the first writer in

English to have 'grappled decisively with Italian language, literature and culture' and that he was followed in this passion for all things Italian by John Milton, Percy Bysshe Shelley, and James Joyce – to which I would add D. H. Lawrence and Ernest Hemingway.

Thanks to the New Chaucer Society and the late Derek Brewer, the two-volume edition of *Sources and Analogues of the Canterbury Tales* issued in 2002 and 2005 revised and updated the version that was first published in 1941. I have used the Middle English texts of *The Riverside Chaucer* and Jill Mann's edition of the *Canterbury Tales* (Penguin, 2005) as my sources for the Tales, but I have also quoted from modern versions by Nevill Coghill (Penguin, 2003) and Peter Ackroyd (Penguin, 2010). Instead of adding footnotes, I have listed my sources in detail in the Bibliography.

While taking a broad approach to what Chaucer drew from Italy and what he would have seen there, I have drawn on some of the many scholarly studies of Chaucer published over the past one hundred years and more. I am most grateful to Marion Turner, Professor of English Literature at Oxford University and Tutorial Fellow in English at Jesus College, Oxford, who read a draft of *Chaucer's Italy,* offered expert and perceptive advice, and suggested amendments.

My thanks too for their help and encouragement to Piero Boitani, professor of Comparative Literature at La Sapienza University, Rome; Peter Brown, professor of Medieval English Literature at the University of Kent in Canterbury; Helen Fulton, professor of Medieval Literature at the University of Bristol; Helen Cooper, emeritus professor of Medieval and

Renaissance English at the University of Cambridge; Nick Havely, emeritus professor of English and Related Literature at the University of York; Jill Mann, former professor of Medieval and Renaissance English at the University of Cambridge and emeritus professor of English at the University of Notre Dame; Wendy Childs, emeritus professor of Later Medieval History at the University of Leeds; and Chris Wickham, emeritus Chichele professor of Medieval History at the University of Oxford and emeritus professor of Medieval History at the University of Birmingham.

My thanks too to Harry Hall, Alice Horne, and especially Jo Stimfield at Haus Publishing for their backing, encouragement, and editing skills. Above all I thank my wife Julia, for her knowledge of all things Italian and for being an unfailing source of support and insight as well as my travelling companion. Needless to say, any errors remaining are my own.

Bibliography

Journals I have consulted include the *Journal of Medieval History*, published by Elsevier, the Netherlands; *The Chaucer Review*, Penn State University; *Studies in the Age of Chaucer*, Yearbook of the New Chaucer Society, University of Notre Dame; *Publications of the Modern Language Association of America (PMLA)*; *Speculum*, University of Chicago; *Medieval Forum*, San Francisco State University; *The Journal of English and Germanic Philology*, University of Illinois; *Modern Language Notes*, Johns Hopkins University; *Modern Philology*, University of Chicago; *Medium Ævum*, Society for the Study of Medieval Languages and Literature; *Romance Notes*, University of North Carolina; *Annali d'Italianistica*, Arizona State University; and *Italica*, the Journal of the American Association of Teachers of Italian.

Euan Roger's online extracts from the National Archives are a valuable resource (*The Civil Servant's Tale, Geoffrey Chaucer in the Archives*, National Archives Blog, 30 October 2017, 27 November 2017 and 2 January 2018), as is Harvard's *Geoffrey Chaucer Website*: chaucer.fas.harvard.edu. The translation of Petrarch's version of the tale of Patient Griselda is taken from *Petrarch: The First Modern Scholar and Man of Letters* by H. Robinson and H. W. Rolfe, New York, 1899.

Books

Ackroyd, Peter, *Chaucer*, Chatto and Windus, 2004.

Akbari, Suzanne Conklin, and Simpson, James (eds), *The Oxford Handbook of Chaucer*, Oxford University Press, 2020.

Allen, Mark, and Amsel, Stephanie, *Annotated Chaucer Bibliography 1997–2010*, Manchester University Press, 2015.

Barański, Zygmunt G., and McLaughlin, Martin, *Italy's Three Crowns: Reading Dante, Petrarch and Boccaccio*, Bodleian Library, 2007.

Bartlett, Kenneth R., *The Civilization of the Italian Renaissance: A Sourcebook*, D. C. Heath and Co, 1992.

Benes, Carrie E. (ed), *A Companion to Medieval Genoa*, Brill, 2018.

Benson, C. David, and Robertson, Elizabeth (eds), *Chaucer's Religious Tales*, D. S. Brewer, 1990.

Benson, C. David, *Imagined Romes: The Ancient City and its Stories in Middle English Poetry*, Pennsylvania State University Press, 2019.

Benson, Larry D., Pratt, Robert, and Robinson F. N. (eds), *The Riverside Chaucer*, Houghton Mifflin, 1987.

Biggs, Frederick, *Chaucer's Decameron and the Origin of the Canterbury Tales*, D. S. Brewer, 2017.

Bishop, Morris, *Petrarch and his World*, Kennikat Press, 1973.

Blandeau, Agnès, *Pasolini, Chaucer and Boccaccio: Two Medieval Texts and their Translation to Film*, McFarland and Co, 2006.

Boccaccio, Giovanni, *Decameron*, Bietti, 1966.

Boccaccio, Giovanni, *Decameron (Wordsworth Classics of World Literature)*, Wordsworth Editions, 2005.

Boccaccio, Giovanni, *Tales from the Decameron*, Peter Hainsworth (trans), Penguin, 2015.

Boitani, Piero, *Chaucer and Boccaccio*, Society for the Study of Medieval Languages and Literature, 1977.

Boitani, Piero (ed), *Chaucer and the Italian Trecento*, Cambridge University Press, 1983.

Boitani, Piero, *Geoffrey Chaucer: Opere*, Vincenzo La Gioia (trans), Einaudi, 2000.

Boitani, Piero, and Mann, Jill, *The Cambridge Companion to Chaucer*, Cambridge University Press, 2004.

Bosco, Umberto, *Francesco Petrarca*, Editori Laterza, 1961.

Branca, Vittore (ed), *Tutte le Opere di Giovanni Boccaccio*, Mondadori, 1976.

Brewer, Derek, *An Introduction to Chaucer*, Longman, 1984.

Brewer, Derek, *Chaucer and his World*, Methuen, 1978.

Brown, Peter (ed), *A Companion to Chaucer*, Blackwell, 2002.

Brown, Peter (ed), *A New Companion to Chaucer*, Blackwell, 2019.

Brown, Peter, *Geoffrey Chaucer*, Oxford University Press, 2011.

Brown, Peter, *Reading Chaucer: Selected Essays*, Peter Lang, 2013.

Caferro, William, *John Hawkwood: An English Mercenary in Fourteenth-Century Italy*, Johns Hopkins University Press, 2006.

Carr, Helen, *The Red Prince: The Life of John of Gaunt, Duke of Lancaster*, Oneworld Publications, 2021.

Chaucer, Geoffrey, *The Canterbury Tales*, Neville Coghill (trans), Penguin Classics, 2003.

Chaucer, Geoffrey, and Ackroyd, Peter, *The Canterbury Tales: A Retelling by Peter Ackroyd*, Penguin, 2010.

Chesterton, G. K., *Chaucer*, Faber and Faber, 1932.

Chiarini, Cino, *Dalle Novelle di Canterbury di G. Chaucer*, Zanichelli, 1897.

Chiarini, Cino, *Da una imitazione inglese della Divina Commedia: la Casa della Fama di Chaucer*, Laterza e Figli, 1902.

Clarke, K. P., *Chaucer and Italian Textuality*, Oxford University Press, 2011.

Cooper, Helen, *The Structure of the Canterbury Tales*, Duckworth, 1983.

Correale, Robert M., and Hamel, Mary, *Sources and Analogues of the Canterbury Tales*, D. S. Brewer, 2002–5.

Crow, Martin M., and Olsen, Clair C., *Chaucer: Life-Records*, Clarendon Press, 1966.

Cummings, Hubertis M., *The Indebtedness of Chaucer's Works to the Italian Works of Boccaccio*, Forgotten Books, 2018.

Edwards, Robert, *Chaucer and Boccaccio: Antiquity and Modernity*, Palgrave Macmillan, 2002.

Ellis, Steve (ed), *Chaucer: An Oxford Guide*, Oxford University Press, 2005.

Falk, Seb, *The Light Ages: A Medieval Journey of Discovery*, Penguin, 2020.

Fein, Susanna, and Raybin, David, *Chaucer: Contemporary Approaches*, Penn State University Press, 2010.

Fulton, Helen (ed), *Chaucer and Italian Culture*, University of Wales Press, 2021.

Fulton, Helen, and Campopiano, Michele (eds), *Anglo-Italian Cultural Relations in the Later Middle Ages*, Boydell and Brewer, 2018.

Gaston, Kara, *Reading Chaucer in Time: Literary Formation in England and Italy*, Oxford University Press, 2020.

Ginsberg, Warren, *Chaucer's Italian Tradition*, University of Michigan Press, 2002.

Goodman, Anthony, *John of Gaunt: The Exercise of Princely Power in Fourteenth-Century Europe*, Routledge, 2013.

Gregorovius, Ferdinand, *History of the City of Rome in the Middle Ages*, G. Bell, 1894.

Havely, Nick, *Chaucer's Boccaccio: Sources for Troilus and the Knight's and Franklin's Tales*, Boydell and Brewer, 1980.

Havely, Nick, *Dante's British Public: Readers and Texts from the Fourteenth Century to the Present*, Oxford University Press, 2014.

Hirsch, John C., *Chaucer and the Canterbury Tales: A Short Introduction*, Blackwell, 2003.

Hobday, Charles, *A Golden Ring: English Poets in Florence from 1373 to the Present Day*, Peter Owen, 1997.

Howard, Donald, *Chaucer and the Medieval World*, Weidenfeld and Nicholson, 1987.

Hulbert, James Root, *Chaucer's Official Life*, G. Banta Pub. Co, 1912.

Hussey, Stanley Stewart, *Chaucer: An Introduction*, Methuen, 1971.

Hutton, Edward, *Giovanni Boccaccio: A Biographical Study*, Good Press, 2019.

Hyde, John Kenneth, *Society and Politics in Medieval Italy: The Evolution of the Civil Life 1000–1350*, Palgrave Macmillan, 1973.

Johnson, Ian (ed), *Geoffrey Chaucer in Context*, Cambridge University Press, 2019.

Jones, Terry, *Chaucer's Knight: The Portrait of a Medieval Mercenary*, Weidenfeld, 1980.

Jones, Terry, et al., *Who Murdered Chaucer? A Medieval Mystery*, Methuen, 2003.

Kelly, M. J., *Chaucer and the Cult of St Valentine*, Brill, 1986.

King, Ross, *Brunelleschi's Dome: The Story of the Great Cathedral in Florence*, Vintage Publishing, 2008.

Kirkham, Victoria, and Maggi, Armando, *Petrarch: A Critical Guide to the Complete Works*, University of Chicago Press, 2012.

Koff, Leonard Michael, and Schildgen, Brenda Deen, *The Decameron and the Canterbury Tales: New Essays on an Old Question*, Associated University Presses, 2000.

Labarge, Margaret Wade, *Medieval Travellers: The Rich and Restless*, Hamish Hamilton, 1982.

Lounsbury, Thomas, *Studies in Chaucer*, Harper and Brothers, 1891.

Mann, Jill, *Feminizing Chaucer*, Boydell and Brewer, 2002.

Mantel, Hilary, *The Mirror and the Light*, Fourth Estate, 2020.

McCormack, Francis, *Chaucer and the Culture of Dissent: The Lollard Context and Subtext of the Parson's Tale*, Four Courts Press, 2007.

McLaughlin, Martin, Panizza, Letizia, and Hainsworth, Peter (eds), *Petrarch in Britain: Interpreters, Imitators and Translators over 700 Years*, Oxford University Press, 2007.

Negru, Catalin, *History of the Apocalypse*, Lulu Press, 2015.

Nicolle, David, *The History of Medieval Life: A Guide to Life from 1000 to 1500 AD*, Chancellor Press, 2000.

Ó Cuilleanáin, Cormac, *Religion and Clergy in Boccaccio's Decameron*, Edizioni di Storia e Litteratura, 1984.

Origo, Iris, *The Merchant of Prato: Daily Life in a Medieval Italian City*, Jonathan Cape, 1957.

Patterson, Lee, *Geoffrey Chaucer's The Canterbury Tales: A Casebook*, Oxford University Press, 2007.

Pearsall, Derek, *The Life of Geoffrey Chaucer: A Critical Biography*, Blackwell, 1994.

Phillips, Helen (ed), *Chaucer and Religion*, D. S. Brewer, 2010.

Picard, Liza, *Chaucer's People: Everyday Lives in the Middle Ages*, Orion, 2017.

Plöger, Karsten, *England and the Avignon Popes: The Practice of Diplomacy in Late Medieval Europe*, Legenda, 2005.

Power, Eileen, *Medieval People*, Dover Publications, 2003.

Rigby, Stephen Henry, and Minnis, Alistair J., *Historians on Chaucer: The General Prologue to the Canterbury Tales*, Oxford University Press, 2014.

Robinson, J. H. and Rolfe, H. W., *Petrarch: The First*

Modern Scholar and Man of Letters, G.P. Putnam's Sons, 1899.

Root, Robert K., *The Poetry of Chaucer*, Gordon Press, 1972.

Rossiter, William, *Chaucer and Petrarch*, Boydell and Brewer, 2010.

Rowland, Beryl, *Companion to Chaucer Studies*, Oxford University Press, 1968.

Rudd, Gillian, *The Complete Critical Guide to Geoffrey Chaucer*, Routledge, 2001.

Salter, Elizabeth, *Chaucer: 'The Knight's Tale' and 'The Clerk's Tale'*, Edward Arnold, 1962.

Sapori, Armando, *The Italian Merchant in the Middle Ages*, Patricia Ann Kennen (trans), Norton, 1970.

Saul, Nigel, *Richard II*, Yale University Press, 1997.

Saul, Nigel, *The Batsford Companion to Medieval England*, Batsford Academic and Educational Ltd, 1983.

Saunders, Frances Stonor, *Hawkwood: Diabolical Englishman*, Faber and Faber, 2004.

Schless, Howard H., *Chaucer and Dante: A Revaluation*, Pilgrim Books, 1984.

Seton, Anya, *Katherine*, Houghton Mifflin, 1954.

Skeat, W. W., *The Complete Works of Geoffrey Chaucer*, Clarendon Press, 1899.

Speirs, John, *Chaucer the Maker*, Faber and Faber, 1951.

Spufford, Peter, *Power and Profit: The Merchant in Medieval Europe*, Thames and Hudson, 2002.

Strohm, Paul, *The Poet's Tale: Chaucer and the Year that Made the Canterbury Tales*, Profile Books, 2015.

Sumption, Jonathan, *The Hundred Years War*, Faber and Faber, Vols 1–4, 1990–2015.

Tatlock, John, *The Mind and Art of Chaucer*, Gordian Press, 1966.

Thompson, N. S., *Chaucer, Boccaccio and the Debate of Love: A Comparative Study of the Decameron and the Canterbury Tales*, Oxford University Press, 1996.

Tuchman, Barbara, *A Distant Mirror: The Calamitous Fourteenth Century*, Alfred A. Knopf, 1978.

Turner, Marion, *Chaucer: A European Life*, Princeton University Press, 2019.

Waley, Daniel, *The Italian City-Republics*, Longman, 1988.

Wallace, David, *Chaucer and the Early Writings of Boccaccio*, D. S. Brewer, 1985.

Wallace, David, *Chaucerian Polity: Absolutist Lineages and Associational Forms in England and Italy*, Stanford University Press, 1997.

Wallace, David, *Geoffrey Chaucer: A Very Short Introduction*, Oxford University Press, 2019.

Wallace, David, *Premodern Places: Calais to Surinam, Chaucer to Aphra Behn*, Blackwell, 2004.

Weir, Alison, *Katherine Swynford: The Story of John of Gaunt and his Scandalous Duchess*, Jonathan Cape, 2007.

Wickham, Chris, *Medieval Europe*, Yale University Press, 2017.

Wilkins, E. H., *Life of Petrarch*, University of Chicago Press, 1961.

Wilson, A. N., *Dante in Love*, Atlantic Books, 2011.

Wright, Herbert G., *Boccaccio in England: From Chaucer to Tennyson*, Athlone, 1957.

Articles and book chapters

Anderson, David, 'The Italian Background to Chaucer's Epic Similes', *Annali d'Italianistica*, Vol 12, 1994.

Barisone, Ermanno, 'Demolire e Ricostruire Chaucer', Paola Carbone (ed), *Congenialita e Traduzione*, Mimesis, 1998.

Beidler, Peter G., 'Chaucer's Merchant's Tale and the Decameron', *Italica*, Vol 50, No 2, Summer 1973.

Beidler, Peter G., 'Just Say Yes, Chaucer Knew the *Decameron*: or, Bringing the Shipman's Tale out of Limbo', Leonard Michael Koff and Brenda Deen Schildgen (eds), *The Decameron and the Canterbury tales: New Essays on an Old Question*, Fairleigh Dickinson University Press, 2000.

Bennett, J. A. W., 'Chaucer, Dante and Boccaccio', Piero Boitani (ed), *Chaucer and the Italian Trecento*, Cambridge University Press, 1983.

Bestul, Thomas H., 'Did Chaucer Live at 177 Thames Street? The Chaucer Life-Records and the Site of Chaucer's London Home', *The Chaucer Review*, Vol 43, No 1, 2008.

Bernardo, Aldo S., 'Petrarch's Attitude Toward Dante', *Publications of the Modern Language Association of America*, Vol 70, No 3, June 1955.

Biggs, Frederick, 'The Miller's Tale and Decameron III.4', *The Journal of English and Germanic Philology*, Vol 108, No 1, January 2009.

Boitani, Piero, 'Chaucer Translates from Italian', Denis
    Renevey and Christiana Whitehead (eds), *Lost in
    Translation?*, Brepols Publishers, 2009.

Boitani, Piero, 'Introduction', Piero Boitani (ed), *Chaucer
    and the Italian Trecento*, Cambridge University Press, 1983.

Bosco, Umberto, 'Introduzione', Giovanni Boccaccio,
    Decameron, Bietti, 1966.

Braddy, Haldeen, 'Chaucer, Alice Perrers and Cecily
    Chaumpaigne', *Speculum*, Vol 52, No 4, October 1977.

Braddy, Haldeen, 'Chaucer and Dame Alice Perrers',
    Speculum, Vol 21, No 2, April 1946.

Braddy, Haldeen, 'New Documentary Evidence Concerning
    Chaucer's Mission to Lombardy', *Modern Language Notes*,
    Vol 48, No 8, December 1933.

Bradley, Helen, '"Saluti da Londra": Italian Merchants
    in the City of London in the Late Fourteenth and
    Early Fifteenth Centuries', Helen Fulton and Michele
    Campopiano (eds), *Anglo-Italian Cultural Relations in the
    Later Middle Ages*, Boydell and Brewer, 2018.

Bright, J. W., 'Chaucer and Lollius', *Publications of the
    Modern Language Association of America*, No 19, 1903.

Cannon, Christopher, 'Chaucer's Rape: Uncertainty's
    Certainties', *Studies in the Age of Chaucer*, Vol 22, 2000.

Cannon, Christopher, '*Raptus* in the Chaumpaigne Release
    and a Newly Discovered Document Concerning the Life
    of Geoffrey Chaucer', *Speculum*, Vol 68, No 1, January
    1993.

Childs, Wendy, 'Anglo-Italian Contacts in the Fourteenth

Century', Piero Boitani (ed), *Chaucer and the Italian Trecento*, Cambridge University Press, 1983.

Cioffi, Caron, 'The First Italian Essay on Chaucer', *The Chaucer Review*, Vol 22, No 1, Summer 1987.

Clarke, K. P., 'Chaucer and Italy: Contexts and/or Sources', *Literature Compass*, Vol 8, No 8, August 2011.

Clarke, K. P., 'The Italian Tradition', Ian Johnson (ed), *Geoffrey Chaucer in Context*, Cambridge University Press, 2019.

Coleman, William E., 'Chaucer, the Teseida and the Visconti Library at Pavia: A Hypothesis', *Medium Ævum*, Vol 51, No 1, 1982.

Cook, Albert Stanburrough, 'The Last Months of Chaucer's Earliest Patron', *Transactions of the Connecticut Academy of Arts and Sciences*, Vol 21, December 1916.

Cooper, Helen, 'The Classical Background', Steve Ellis (ed), *Chaucer: An Oxford Guide*, Oxford University Press, 2005.

Coulter, Cornelia C., 'Boccaccio and the Cassinese Manuscripts of the Laurentian Library', *Classical Philology*, Vol 43, No 4, October 1948.

Dale, Sharon, '*Contra damnationis filios*: The Visconti in fourteenth-century papal diplomacy', *Journal of Medieval History*, Vol 33, No 1, March 2007.

Davis, Norman, 'Language and Versification', Larry D. Benson (ed), *The Riverside Chaucer*, Oxford University Press, 1988.

Delasanta, Rodney, 'Chaucer, Pavia and the Ciel d'Oro', *Medium Ævum*, Vol 54, No 1, 1985.

Dorris, George E., 'The First Italian Criticism of Chaucer

and Shakespeare', *Romance Notes*, Vol 6, No 2, Spring 1965.

Dunn, Caroline, 'The Language of Ravishment in Medieval England', *Speculum*, Vol 86, No 1, January 2011.

Edwards, Robert, 'Italy', Susanna Fein and David Raybin (eds), *Chaucer: Contemporary Approaches*, Penn State University Press, 2010.

Evans, Ruth, 'Chaucer's Life', Steve Ellis (ed), *Chaucer: An Oxford Guide*, Oxford University Press, 2005.

Farnham, Willard, 'England's Discovery of the Decameron', *Publications of the Modern Language Association of America*, Vol 39, No 1, March 1924.

Fehrman, Craig T., 'Did Chaucer Read the Wycliffite Bible?', *The Chaucer Review*, Vol 42, No 2, 2007.

Finlayson, John, 'Petrarch, Boccaccio and Chaucer's Clerk's Tale', *Studies in Philology*, Vol 97, No 3, Summer 2000.

Galloway, Andrew, 'Chaucer's life and literary "profession"', Ian Johnson (ed), *Geoffrey Chaucer in Context*, Cambridge University Press, 2019.

Galway, Margaret, 'Chaucer's Journeys in 1368', *Times Literary Supplement*, 4 April 1958.

Georgianna, Linda, 'Anticlericalism in Boccaccio and Chaucer: The Bark and the Bite', Leonard Michael Koff and Brenda Deen Schildgen (eds), *The Decameron and the Canterbury Tales: New Essays on an Old Question*, Associated University Presses, 2000.

Georgianna, Linda, 'The Protestant Chaucer', C. David Benson and Elizabeth Robertson (eds), *Chaucer's Religious Tales*, D. S. Brewer, 1990.

Gross, Karen Elizabeth, 'Chaucer's Silent Italy', *Studies in Philology*, Vol 109, No 1, Winter 2012.

Hagiioannu, Michael, 'Giotto's Bardi Chapel Frescoes and Chaucer's House of Fame: Influence, Evidence and Interpretations', *The Chaucer Review*, Vol 36, No 1, 2001.

Haines, Charles, 'Patient Griselda and Matta Bestialitade', *Quaderni d'italianistica*, Vol 6, No 2, January 1985.

Harley, Marta Powell, 'Geoffrey Chaucer, Cecilia Chaumpaigne and Alice Perrers: A Closer Look', *The Chaucer Review*, Vol 28, No 1, 1993.

Havely, Nick, 'Chaucer, Boccaccio and the Friars', Piero Boitani (ed), *Chaucer and the Italian Trecento*, Cambridge University Press, 1983.

Havely, Nick, 'The Italian Background', Steve Ellis (ed), *Chaucer: An Oxford Guide*, Oxford University Press, 2005.

Hunt, Edwin S., 'A New Look at the Dealings of the Bardi and Peruzzi with Edward III', *The Journal of Economic History*, Vol 50, No 1, March 1990.

Kaiser, Melanie L., and Dean, James M., 'Chaucer and the Early Church', *Medieval Forum*, Vol 5, January 2006.

Kamowski, William, 'Chaucer and Wyclif: God's Miracles Against the Clergy's Magic', *The Chaucer Review*, Vol 37, No 1, 2002.

Kirkpatrick, Robin, 'The Wake of the Commedia: Chaucer's Canterbury Tales and Boccaccio's Decameron', Piero Boitani (ed), *Chaucer and the Italian Trecento*, Cambridge University Press, 1983.

Kuhl, E. P., 'Why was Chaucer sent to Milan in 1378?', *Modern Language Notes*, Vol 62, No 1, January 1947.

Larner, John, 'Chaucer's Italy', Piero Boitani (ed), *Chaucer and the Italian Trecento*, Cambridge University Press, 1983.

Lewis, C. S., 'What Chaucer Really Did to Il Filostrato', *Essays and Studies by Members of the English Association*, Vol 17, 1932.

Longsworth, Robert, 'The Wife of Bath and the Samaritan Woman', *The Chaucer Review*, Vol 34, No 4, 2000.

Machan, Tim William, 'Texts', Peter Brown (ed), *A Companion to Chaucer*, Blackwell, 2002.

Manly, John M., 'Chaucer's Mission to Lombardy', *Modern Language Notes*, Vol 49, No 4, April 1934.

Mather, Frank Jewett Jr, 'An Inedited Document Concerning Chaucer's First Italian Journey', *Modern Language Notes*, Vol 11, No 7, November 1896.

Mather, Frank Jewett Jr, 'On the Asserted Meeting of Chaucer and Petrarch', *Modern Language Notes*, Vol 12, No 1, January 1897.

Mazzotta, Giuseppe, 'Foreword', Leonard Michael Koff and Brenda Deen Schildgen (eds), *The Decameron and the Canterbury Tales: New Essays on an Old Question*, Associated University Presses, 2000.

McCormack, Frances, 'Chaucer and Lollardy', Helen Phillips (ed), *Chaucer and Religion*, D. S. Brewer, 2010.

McGrady, Donald, 'Chaucer and the *Decameron* Reconsidered', *The Chaucer Review*, Vol 12, No 1, Summer 1977.

Ó Cuilleanáin, Cormac, 'Introduction', Giovanni Boccaccio, *Decameron*, Wordsworth, 2004.

Ormond, W. M., 'Who Was Alice Perrers?', *The Chaucer Review*, Vol 40, No 3, 2006.

Parks, George B., 'The Route of Chaucer's First Journey to Italy', *English Literary History*, Vol 16, No 3, September 1949.

Power, Eileen, *The Wool Trade in English Medieval History*, James Ford Lecture in British History, Oxford University, 1939.

Pratt, John H., 'Was Chaucer's Knight Really a Mercenary?', *The Chaucer Review*, Vol 22, No 1, Summer 1987.

Pratt, Robert Armstrong, 'Chaucer and the Visconti Libraries', *English Literary History*, Vol 6, No 3, September 1939.

Pratt, Robert Armstrong, 'Chaucer's Shipman's Tale and Sercambi', *Modern Language Notes*, Vol 55, No 2, February 1940.

Pratt, Robert Armstrong, 'Chaucer's Use of the Teseida,' *Publications of the Modern Language Association of America*, Vol 62, No 3, September 1947.

Pratt, Robert Armstrong, 'Conjectures Regarding Chaucer's Manuscript of the Teseida', *Studies in Philology*, Vol 42, No 4, October 1945.

Pratt, Robert Armstrong, 'Geoffrey Chaucer Esq and Sir John Hawkwood,' *English Literary History*, Vol 16, No 3, September 1949.

Rickert, Edith, 'Chaucer Abroad in 1368', *Modern Philology*, Vol 25, No 4, May 1928.

Ruggiers, Paul, 'The Italian Influence on Chaucer', Beryl

Rowland (ed), *Companion to Chaucer Studies*, Oxford University Press, 1968.

Schless, Howard, 'Transformations: Chaucer's Use of Italian', Derek Brewer (ed), *Geoffrey Chaucer*, G. Bell, 1974.

Schofield, William Henry, 'Chaucer's Franklin's Tale', *Publications of the Modern Language Association of America*, Vol 16, No 3, 1901.

Seal, Samantha Katz, 'Chaucer's Other *Wyf*: Philippa Chaucer, the Critics and the English Canon', *The Chaucer Review*, Vol 54, No 3, 2019.

Sobecki, Sebastian, 'Wards and Widows: Troilus and Criseyde and New Documents on Chaucer's Life,' *English Literary History*, Vol 86, No 2, Summer 2019.

Strohm, Paul, 'Fleeced!', *Lapham's Quarterly*, 29 April 2015.

Strohm, Paul, 'Who was Chaucer?', *The Guardian*, 24 January 2015.

Tatlock, John, 'The Duration of Chaucer's Visits to Italy', *Journal of English and Germanic Philology*, Vol 12, No 1, January 1913.

Wallace, David, 'Chaucer and Boccaccio's Early Writings', Piero Boitani (ed), *Chaucer and the Italian Trecento*, Cambridge University Press, 1983.

Wallace, David, 'Chaucer's Italian Inheritance', Piero Boitani and Jill Mann (eds), *The Cambridge Companion to Chaucer*, Cambridge University Press, 2004.

Wallace, David, 'Italy', Peter Brown (ed), *A Companion to Chaucer*, Blackwell, 2002.

Wallace, David, 'Chaucer's Continental Inheritance: the

Early Poems and Troilus and Crysede', Piero Boitani and Jill Mann (eds), *The Cambridge Companion to Chaucer*, Cambridge University Press, 2004.

Watson, Nicholas, 'Christian Ideologies', Peter Brown (ed), *A Companion to Chaucer*, Blackwell, 2002.

Welch, Evelyn Samuels, 'Galeazzo Maria Sforza and the Castello di Pavia, 1469', *The Art Bulletin*, Vol 71, No 3, September 1989.

Windeatt, Barry, 'Chaucer and the Filostrato', Piero Boitani (ed), *Chaucer and the Italian Trecento*, Cambridge University Press, 1983.